River Road
RAMBLER RETURNS

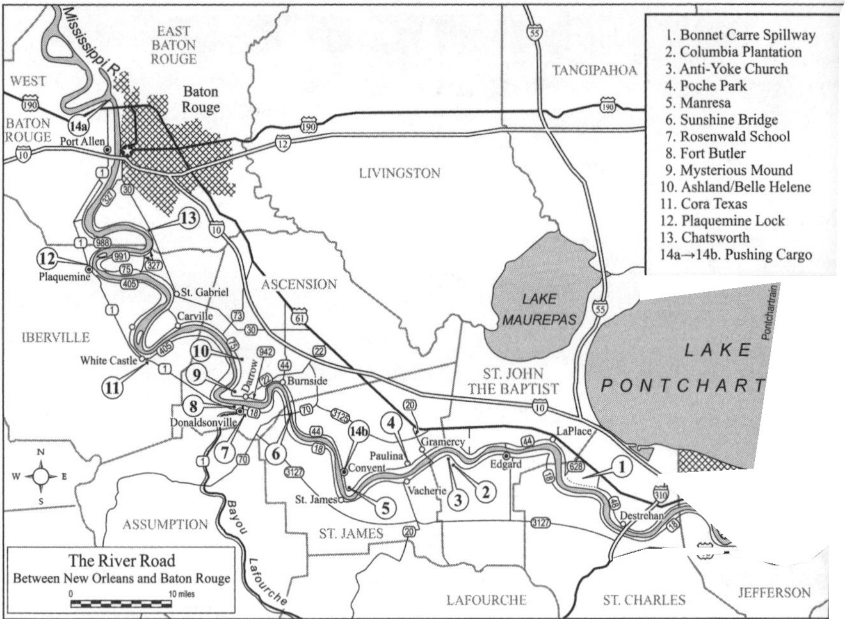

Map by Mary Lee Eggart

River Road RAMBLER RETURNS

More Curiosities along Louisiana's Historic Byway

Mary Ann Sternberg

Illustrations by Elizabeth Randall Neely

Louisiana State University Press
Baton Rouge

Published with the assistance of the Borne Fund

Published by Louisiana State University Press

Manufactured in the United States of America
First printing

Designer: Laura Roubique Gleason
Typeface: Calluna
Printer and binder: Sheridan Books, Inc.

Library of Congress Cataloging-in-Publication Data

Names: Sternberg, Mary Ann, author. | Neely, Elizabeth Randall, illustrator.
Title: River Road rambler returns : more curiosities along Louisiana's historic byway / Mary Ann Sternberg ; illustrations by Elizabeth Randall Neely.
Description: Baton Rouge : Louisiana State University Press, [2018]
Identifiers: LCCN 2018001238 | ISBN 978-0-8071-6928-5 (cloth : alk. paper) | ISBN 978-0-8071-6954-4 (pdf) | ISBN 978-0-8071-6929-2 (epub)
Subjects: LCSH: River Road (La.)—History. | River Road (La.)—History, Local. | River Road (La.)—Social life and customs. | Historic sites—Louisiana—River Road.
Classification: LCC F377.R58 S857 2018 | DDC 976.3/18—dc23
LC record available at https://lccn.loc.gov/2018001238

The paper in this book meets the guidelines for permanence and durability of the Committee on Production Guidelines for Book Longevity of the Council on Library Resources. ♾

CONTENTS

PREFACE

For more than two decades, I have rambled the River Road and enjoyed (almost) every minute.

I have sought to challenge the common but much-too-narrow conception of the River Road as merely a parade of antebellum plantation homes open to the public. While these rewarding museums are the most visible and accessible attractions, I discovered early that the River Road was infinitely more historic, complex, and rewarding than simply a mid-nineteenth-century trail of grand mansions. It is, instead, a messy patchwork landscape, created by three hundred years of settlement. Prehistoric and historic Native Americans, French, Spanish, Germans, Creoles, Cajuns, slaves from Africa and the West Indies, free people of color, Anglo-Americans, Italians, and others have lived here, leaving their influences and traditions. This produced a jambalaya setting where rich history shoulders the irrelevant, the beautiful is sometimes jammed next to the derelict, and the elegant and gritty coexist, making rambling this area a very rich experience indeed.

As with my previous River Road books, I've maintained a constant geography that, at first glance, may seem arbitrary. My focus is the approximately one-hundred-mile-long corridor that traces both banks of the Mississippi River between New Orleans and Baton Rouge, from the Jefferson/St. Charles parish line into parts of East and West Baton Rouge Parishes. I consciously omitted the greater New Orleans area and most of Baton Rouge because I didn't want to duplicate the many fine and detailed books that already exist about these regions.

I wish I had kept count of how many excursions I've made to the River Road over these twenty-plus years. Although it is very close to my home in Baton Rouge, I have followed Walker Percy's advice to "explore your neighborhood" and, in doing so, found that each trip seemed like a true excursion, filled with discovery and the feeling of being "away." When I go rambling along the River Road, I usually carry a notepad and always pack a dedicated curiosity and sense of humor. The latter, especially, is required in an area that is abundantly quirky.

Sometimes I've stayed out on the road for a night or two; on other occasions I've dashed out only for the day. Regardless, I've always found both entertainment and good eating. I've enjoyed a Creole breakfast in a B&B, an oyster poboy lunch at a derelict-looking gas station, and a quasi-elegant dinner in a pleasant restaurant setting. It is all out there.

I am writing this second collection of Rambler stories to again cast a spotlight on sites that have intrigued me either because they are truly unique or because they seem worthy of more attention than they usually command. As in the previous Rambler book, each of these fourteen stories is derived from several sources: archival research, to support the history; interviews with generous locals willing to share knowledge of their area; and firsthand observation, noting what I see and, sometimes, what I feel. And, always, a personal bonus is the informal education I've obtained in matters far outside my usual frame of reference—how sugar is milled, for example, or what daily life on a Mississippi River towboat is like.

The stories are grouped somewhat thematically rather than geographically, but the small map of the area included at the front of the book will give you a sense of proximities, in case you wish to ramble from one place to the next.

One of the greatest revelations has been my realization that there are two distinct but connected landscapes that exist along the River Road. On one side of the stalwart levees is the familiar: historic buildings of all kinds—museums, sugar factories, atmospheric old churches and cemeteries—and much more. On the other side is the world of the river, a place unto itself. For, although the Mississippi River has been the centerpiece of this area since first settlement, today we often forget its presence because of the protective earthen banks that keep floods from our doorstep but have rendered the river invisible. This topographical separation is a modern development; for hundreds of years, the river was a constant companion as well as the lifeblood of area residents—their artery of commerce and most dependable means of transportation, a reliable source of fuel and food, even a site for baptisms.

Perhaps, because of this visual separation, I am still surprised at the vastness of the river and its activity. The procession of tugs and towboats, tankers, freighters, and workboats is endless; the banks are lined with an assortment of marine services. Between the levees is a maritime world noisy with hums and rumbles, clanks and groans and hoots. And I am fascinated by the river itself; I often stand on the batture, watching the brown water swirling past, sometimes ferociously, and marvel at its power by the progress of logs and debris racing past. And I've looked for opportunities to ride the historic river as much as I can, a challenge for someone who doesn't own a boat. But the thrill is to be "inside" the river, which I've happily accomplished by ferry, canoe, and even towboat.

As you will note from the stories in this book, I support preservation, whether protecting relics of material culture like old buildings or taking care of the land and the environment. Numerous people along the river—"keepers of the flame," as I think of them— value their history and heritage. Most are senior citizens with firsthand knowledge of old places and old ways, and they hope to pass down their knowledge and culture to the younger generation, the logical heirs. That they have sometimes been met with indifference or a seeming lack of appreciation threatens the River Road and may speed up its transformation. Conversely, however, I have been delighted to find examples of active preservation from sometimes unlikely sources, as several of the stories in this collection reveal.

My preservationist instincts remain rooted in pragmatism, however. The River Road is not a museum under glass but a place of constant change, as it has been for its three centuries of documented history and no doubt in prehistoric times as well. So I willingly embrace changes made with thoughtfulness, when those changes value what is important, yet update and adapt to our twenty-first-century world. Through my rambling, I have come to realize that protection for its own sake is as ill-advised as change without respect for history.

I do hope that these stories give you new insights into little-known places along this historic corridor. And, if they also inspire you to ramble the River Road, I hope you will find as much delight there as I have continued to do.

I

Sacred Spaces

1
The Odyssey of the Anti-Yoke

Rather than sharing a bench with others on the Whitney Plantation tour, I sat down silently on the long wooden pew at the rear of the Antioch Baptist Church. My seatmate was a life-sized child sculpture—dark-skinned, clad in raggedy clothing and a straw hat. He appeared a bit dusty or perhaps just life-worn. The child's expression was pensive, and he looked vulnerable as he stared ahead with eyes that did not pretend to see.

This artistic reproduction of a slave child is one of thirty individualized, three-dimensional artworks—portraits of slave boys and girls—placed around the interior of the old church at Whitney. Some of the sculptures created by artist Woodrow Nash are seated, some stand; some are posed in small groups, others are alone. All have the facial features of young Africans and African Americans and wear the shabby attire—pinafores, sack dresses, overalls—of the mid-nineteenth century's poorest people. They exude innocence and vulnerability, as well as grit.

They are known as the *Children of Whitney.*

I sat on the pew and looked around the sanctuary as our tour guide talked, then punched on an introductory video about the museum. But I paid scant attention to the television monitor, instead regarding the sculpture boy on my bench.

The slave children sculptures and the refurbished old church are parts of a unique River Road plantation complex that John Cummings created after buying the old Whitney Plantation in 1999. His vision: to create "the only plantation museum in Louisiana with a focus on slavery," at this historic sugar estate that used slave labor until emancipation. Cummings's intention seemed to be to unsettle his museum visitors, to persuade folks who paid the entrance fee to dwell on the meaning of slavery. In interviews he gave soon after the Whitney opened, he told a reporter that he wanted to honor the humanity and culture of the enslaved people who had been transported here to support the economic system.

He delivers this message throughout the far-ranging exhibits across the grounds. But, to me, nothing was more poignant or affecting than the powerfully wrought sculptures of slave children, casually arranged in a perfect setting: a church originally built for their own use by a community of freed slaves.

The newly emancipated men and women who lived in east-bank St. James Parish celebrated their freedom by forming an organization for burials called the Anti-Yoke Society. But they soon wanted a formal place to worship and purchased land on a short, dead-end street in the tiny community of Paulina. By 1868, or perhaps 1870, these free people had constructed a small neo-Gothic building, infused with love. Its craftsmanship was striking, especially the exterior, which was clad in decorative, carefully lapped shingles in a complicated design, and enhanced with pointed Gothic windows and a stepped belfry. The interior was clean-lined and spare with little decoration, save the basic elements of the Baptist faith. The congregants named their new church Antioch, which sounded somewhat like Anti-Yoke but actually referred to the town mentioned in the Acts of the Apostles where the followers of Christ were first called Christians. For many years, the Antioch Baptist Church was one of the few black churches in its area.

The builders and their descendants worshiped in the little church for over a century, creating traditions that Pastor Ferdinand Gaines Jr. inherited when he became its cleric in 1973. A dozen or so of his parishioners were direct descendants of the church founders, and the building had been little changed from its origins. The choir, always clad in white (first in dresses and suits, later in robes), ranged across the rear of the small pulpit, leading the congregation in emotional verses of "Jesus Keep Me Near the Cross," "Just a Closer Walk with Thee," and other favorites. The hymns sounded glorious as the voices echoed within the wooden walls.

The baptistry had been built beneath the pulpit, so when a baptism was scheduled, the choir vacated their roost and the floor was removed to expose the baptism pool. Pastor Gaines decided to modernize this rite by moving the baptistry down the nave; the choir could continue singing from the pulpit as the believer was immersed. The pastor also recalled that his little church was quite difficult to heat and cool, despite having central air and heat. "Probably because of the old construction," he told me. "In winter, even with the heat on, people sat with their coats on. And when you baptized someone, the water was sooo cold."

When he assumed the pulpit, the congregation was accustomed to formal services held only twice monthly, when a traveling pastor came from New Orleans. Pastor Gaines initiated weekly services—at ten o'clock sharp, with Sunday school at nine o'clock in the sanctuary. He also encountered a tradition of holding Easter morning services at 3:00 a.m. (to receive Jesus from the tomb, he was told); he modified this to eight o'clock, despite being greeted with the usual grumbles about breaking with custom. He also dismantled the original railing that surrounded the pulpit; it had been built by the founders. More grumbling. But, he felt, it separated him, both physically and spiritually, from his flock.

Nevertheless, for two decades after Pastor Gaines's arrival, membership and attendance at the old Antioch Baptist Church grew. When two hundred congregants had to squeeze into the pews, however, it was clear that they had outgrown the small sanctuary. There was no way to expand the building or the limited parking, which spilled out onto the narrow shoulders along the River Road every Sunday morning.

The solution was to build a new church. The First Community Antioch Baptist Church was completed in 1999 in the town of Lutcher, very near Paulina. It is a grand facility, able to welcome twelve hundred worshipers at one time. The historic little building in Paulina sat empty, inevitably falling into disrepair as time went on. Vandals broke in, smashing the panes of its Gothic windows, battering in the old, wooden doors, and destroying the baptismal pool. The old church of the freed slaves appeared doomed.

But fate ordained otherwise.

Not long after John Cummings had first begun to organize his slave museum, a friend told him about the historic Antioch Baptist Church sitting empty and dilapidated in Paulina. It might be a good addition to his project, the friend suggested, and introduced him to Pastor Gaines. They struck a deal, and John Cummings took title to the old building. In 2001, movers broke the vandalized church into three pieces and carted it across the river to Whitney Plantation.

The church of the freed slaves was reconstructed and refurbished with the same care its builders had taken, though not exactly as most of its living parishioners remembered. A new roof was added and the floor plan was slightly changed, which seemed to render the interior a bit narrower, according to Gaines. The entrance foyer was adapted for the new code for public access, and, although the baptismal pool was not rebuilt, the Gothic-style windows, lost in a previous renovation, were reconstructed after the original frames were discovered. The porch was replaced and vintage pine flooring was laid in the sanctuary, stained a rich brown compatible with the wood of the new pews (the old ones had been given away when the church closed), wainscoting, and chair rails. The rich wood contrasts with the stark white of the walls. Two lines of thin, octagonal columns in a fishtail motif support the arched ceiling. Three delicate wrought-iron chandeliers now hang above the nave; two smaller, more intricate fixtures are suspended over the pulpit, backlit by an arched window. "Overall, it does look very similar," the pastor admitted when I asked what he thought of the renovation. And he was pleased that the old bell now peals again in its renovated belfry.

The old-new Antioch Baptist Church has served as the setting for weddings, family gatherings, and musical performances when Whitney is not open for tours. But it has never again been used for religious services, and probably never will be. This doesn't disturb Pastor Ferdinand Gaines Jr. at all. "The building was saved by its move to Whitney," he observed with some emotion. "I hope it's preserved until the Rapture."

If preserving the Antioch Baptist Church seemed heroic, peopling the space with the slave children sculptures struck me as truly inspired. But this might never have happened had John Cummings missed the booth at the New Orleans Jazz and Heritage Festival where sculptor Woodrow Nash was showing his work. Cummings was intrigued with the African American artist's ceramic pieces and told him about his Whitney project. "John asked me if I thought I could fashion some slave children out of clay," Nash remembered, to tell about life on Whitney Plantation through the eyes of the children who might have lived there.

Nash, who now lives in Akron, Ohio, began his professional artistic career as an illustrator in a New York advertising agency. He began exploring the history of art, the striking breadth of its traditions, and realized that, although numerous African American artists were recognized for paintings and works on paper, few were making statements in three dimensions—creating sculpture. He was attracted to the highly engaging artworks of the fifteenth-century Benin people as well as to imagery from eighteenth-century French art and began creating stylized ceramic sculpture incorporating elements from both aesthetics.

Nash's sculptures are notable for their absence of defined eyes, a Benin technique that struck him as a haunting effect, adding emotion to a piece. "[The Benin] had images of their spiritual leaders on vases and vessels and had vacant eyes, to draw you in," he told me. "When I began to do this, it brought my sculptures to life."

For the sculptures in Cummings's slave memorial, Nash invented a new artistic process. Although his figures appear to be indestructible metal, the three-dimensional portraits are actually hand-built stoneware, the artist's trademark material. The base is clay, mixed with fine iron powder that, when fired at a high temperature, causes the iron to oxidize and form a nonporous finish. To this, he applied a corrosive, to produce the rusty, metallic appearance of the sculptures. Then he overlaid each one individually with automotive glazes, creating the colors of the clothing. Each slave child's distinctive features were modeled from a child visible in post-emancipation photographs, with the Benin-inspired blank eyes.

Each sculpture was also given a name, taken from identifications made from 1930s WPA interviews with elderly black people who had experienced slavery as children or teens. Whitney admission includes a tag on a cord that displays a photograph of one of these sculptures, including the real name of that girl or boy and a bit of their memoir as transcribed by the WPA. My lanyard introduced me to the sculpture girl named Carlyle Stewart.

She is clad in a sleeveless, almost colorless dress that drapes just below her knees. Her head is crowned with short, tight curls; her face is placid; she stands with her arms behind her back. Carlyle Stewart was eighty-seven years old when she told her WPA interviewer, "I was seven years old . . . when we wuz set free." I searched for her in the church and then, as encouraged by Whitney, took my necklace home.

When the introductory video ended, the tour group rose to follow our guide down the aisle of the church, out into the sunlight, to troop around this property dotted with exhibits, monuments, and buildings interpreting slavery. And I noticed, as we silently left the church, that neither the black nor white visitors seemed to pay attention to the slave children sculptures, or to try to find "their" child. It was as if they intended to avert their eyes. Perhaps, I thought, they could not bear to see them.

2
Five Lives on College Point

The exquisite landscape that sprawls behind a handsome fence had always intrigued me—the manicured greensward dotted with ancient live oaks sheltering a series of pristine, white neoclassical buildings. This could be a beautiful private estate with the most colossal big house ever, or certainly the perfect setting for an Old South romance movie.

But a tasteful notice set by the driveway offers assurances that neither casual visitors nor moviemaking would be welcome here. "No Visitors Please, Religious Retreat in Progress," reads the sign that protects the entrance to the Manresa House of Retreats. This beautiful place in the community of Convent is a Catholic center operated by the Jesuit order that welcomes men, both Catholic and not, for spiritual renewal.

I had often observed solitary men of various ages deep in contemplation. I'd seen them seated in well-spaced, old-fashioned wooden lawn chairs, watched them amble down the exquisite oak allée shading Manresa's grounds across River Road by the levee. And I'd talked with friends who had attended retreats at Manresa, experiences they treasured for the facility and the experience, the beauty of the campus, and the feeling that derived from removing themselves from the bustle of everyday life. They had even complimented the south Louisiana-style food shared in a communal dining space. And all of this took place in complete silence.

But none of the retreat attendees I spoke with had sensed any vestiges of the history and tradition that must permeate this campus. They hadn't appreciated that, before its current identity emerged in 1931, the site had been an all-male bastion of learning for almost a century. Some of these same oaks had shaded students, faculty, and staff in a succession of educational institutions for young men. The buildings, so quiet now, would have echoed with the buzz of academic studies and the boisterous voices of rough-and-tumble adolescents. With the grounds serving as fields for competitive sporting activities, the campus would have been predictably noisy, lively, and energetic.

And then, as now, the fairer sex was not welcome.

That is not entirely true anymore, Tim Murphy corrected me. Manresa's general manager, who has overseen the retreat center for almost twenty years, has witnessed various changes recently that included welcoming some school groups chaperoned by both male and female faculty. Manresa has also hosted a few special retreats for New Orleans–based homeless men and women suffering from addictive disorders, he noted. So, yes, women are occasionally on campus. And, yes, I could have a tour of Manresa, for the purpose of writing a story . . . but I must come on one of the (few) days when no retreat was in session.

Which was how, after twenty years of admiring this historic place through the fenceposts along River Road, I would enter and find a campus with a history more complicated and interesting than I'd ever imagined.

The College of Jefferson

In 1831, Creole planters and New Orleans businessmen under the leadership of Governor André Roman (a Creole gentleman himself) determined to establish an educational institution for their sons. They wanted their offspring to "find the means of completing their course of studies without leaving their native land"; the College of Jefferson was the solution. It was named at Roman's suggestion to acknowledge the former president's role in the Louisiana Purchase as well as to show appreciation for his political philosophy. The school would be sited at a perfect location: on Jean Vavasseur's sixty-five-acre plantation on a prominent point on the east bank of St. James Parish, a mere four-hour steamboat ride upriver from New Orleans. In fact, after its founding, steamboat captains began calling the area College Point, and so it is still known.

Roman raised pledges equivalent to $300,000 today. The investors received a state charter for their private institution, then seamlessly became the college's board of directors, ensuring that it would reflect their culture, with instruction taught in French.

The Main Building, completed in 1833, was a formidable three-story, classical revival structure, three hundred feet in length—almost as long as a football field. The building was narrow with large, imposing Doric columns on all sides and a wing connected at the rear. Similarities between the facades of this building and the now-famous Oak Alley plantation house across the river suggested that the two buildings may have shared an architect.

This imposing building was the center of all activities until a pair of small porter's lodges were erected at the main entrance and the President's House, a pint-sized version of a Louisiana plantation house, was constructed on the grounds. The planters soon learned, however, that physically creating a college campus and financially sustaining an institution were separate challenges. When the price of sugar dropped, reducing the planter-investors' incomes, they grew hesitant to honor their pledges, prompting the board to turn to the state of Louisiana for a loan, secured by their mortgage.

State government agreed, and the College of Jefferson began

classes in February of 1834 with sixty-two young men enrolled. Their tuition and board was set at $250, for which they received an education that mingled the spirit of Jeffersonian democracy with regimentation and a veneer of aristocratic tradition. Each student, for example, had to arrive with a usable silver cup.

French was required as the mother tongue of the eight faculty members, but, in deference to the spirit of Mr. Jefferson, French and English were alternated daily as the spoken languages on campus. The library was stocked with representative books on science and literature, and a modern encyclopedia, and all students, Catholic or not, were marched up the River Road to St. Michael's Catholic Church for twice-daily services. The young men were also required to say prayers upon rising and at bedtime.

By 1837, the student body had doubled, requiring additional space, especially a new building for instruction in chemistry and natural philosophy. Again, however, sugar prices were low and board members were reluctant to honor personal pledges, so the directors again approached state government. This time, they sweetened their request by offering a deal: in exchange for the state's assumption of the college's debt, one boy from each of Louisiana's seventeen senatorial districts would be allowed to attend the College of Jefferson free of charge. The state agreed once more; the new building was constructed, and the faculty and staff expanded to twenty-nine, which included a visiting dentist and physician. The next construction project would be completion of a second wing on the Main Building, to increase the College of Jefferson's enrollment to four hundred young men.

When Alexander Hill Everett arrived as the new president of the college in 1841, he stepped from the steamboat onto the grounds of a thriving institution. In his journal he noted the high brick wall along the front of the property, the little gatehouses guarding the main entrance, five brick buildings on campus that included housing for the president and the professors, and labs well stocked with up-to-date instruments. At his (reportedly overlong) invocation, he entreated students to spend their time wisely, to make "the time you pass here . . . one of the most agreeable periods of your life."

Classes were offered on two tracks: classical studies, including Latin and Greek (read in the original), oratory, philosophy, and chemistry; and "special curriculum," or preparation for entering commerce or business administration, without the language requirement. But everyone could participate in arts electives such as dancing and drawing and in recreation such as swimming, walking, fencing, and an early version of ROTC.

The College of Jefferson had rigid rules limiting visitation and correspondence. Spending money was not allowed on campus; tobacco and liquor were prohibited, along with playing cards, betting games, and possession of weapons, "including sword canes." Punishment might be a ration of bread and water for a meal or two or, in especially egregious situations, confinement in a small, seldom-used building called "the prison."

The future looked very bright indeed for the College of Jefferson when, on the morning of March 6, 1842, a fire accidentally started in a laboratory in the new chemistry building. River breezes wafting through open windows fanned the blaze, which quickly spread out of control. By the time the fire was contained, much of the campus had been destroyed. The Main Building was a blackened shell. Only the President's House and porter's lodges survived. No one was killed, but the college was forced to evacuate. All students were ferried home the following day on two steamboats that had pulled up to the (fortunately) undamaged river landing.

Undaunted, Governor Roman and his directors decided to rebuild. The Main Building would be first, but with a reduced footprint. Even this proved a bit too spacious, however, when only fifty-two students matriculated at the college's reopening in March 1844. (This is the building that now serves as Manresa's St. Mary's Hall.)

The revived College of Jefferson never regained the prosperity of its days before the fire, despite such efforts as presenting an honorary degree to southern statesman Henry Clay in 1845. Enrollment remained below breakeven, and the state, with its own financial problems, withdrew support. In desperation, the directors invited the Society of Jesus to take possession of the campus, but the order demurred. And certainly no one could have foreseen that, somewhat ironically, the Jesuits would take over the campus almost a century later as their retreat center.

The College of Jefferson closed its doors in 1847, proud of its efforts and of notable alumni such as Paul Octave Hébert, a Louisiana governor; George Eustis, a congressman and diplomat; and Alfred Roman, son of college founder André Roman, a staff member of General P. G. T. Beauregard during the Civil War.

Louisiana College

Caretakers oversaw the campus for several years after the College of Jefferson closed until in 1853, as yellow fever raged in the Crescent City, a Parisian professor, Louis Dufau, bought the property from the bank. He hoped to recreate his New Orleans institution of higher learning at College Point, in a healthier environment. But after only three years, Dufau's Louisiana College failed, and the bank once again held title to a vacant property.

Jefferson College

Valcour Aime, the legendary mid-nineteenth-century River Road planter, was a creative sugar farmer, a man of grand-scale thinking, and famously rich. He was also André Roman's brother-in-law, and Aime's son Gabriel had been a student at the College of Jefferson. So perhaps Valcour Aime had a soft spot for the institution when he was cajoled into taking over the mortgage and reopening the college. The planter reorganized the administration and turned the property over to his four sons-in-law, advising them to form a corporation, sell shares at $100 each, and raise a pool of $10,000. They were highly successful, allowing them to refurbish the buildings and open the new, renamed Jefferson College on November 1, 1859. It had a new board of directors, a new president and faculty, and sixty young male students, among whom were some "rougher boys," not of the planter class.

Retreatants at Manresa continue to enjoy Valcour Aime's remaining contribution to the campus—the Gothic revival–style chapel which he had built in memory of Gabriel and his daughter Félicie, both victims of yellow fever. It was constructed on a typical cruciform plan, with exterior walls of stucco over brick, finished to look like stone, and pointed lancet windows and pinnacles capped with crosses that contribute to its neo-Gothic style. Architectural historians have dubbed the building "a jewel of ecclesiastical architecture in Louisiana."

The success of Valcour Aime's leadership and that of his sons-in-law was short-lived because, two short years later, Louisiana had seceded from the Union and war talk filled the campus. Students were considering enlisting in the Confederacy when suddenly, after the capture of New Orleans in 1862, the war came to College Point. Federal boats made their way up the Mississippi River and Union troops appropriated the campus for military barracks. Faculty and students fled. The occupying soldiers trashed the buildings, burned library books for fuel, destroyed the labs, and chopped down numerous old oaks. This was heresy enough, but what apparently agitated the directors even more was a rumor that Jefferson College might be used as a school for freedmen. They approached the archbishop of New Orleans, to request that he bring Jefferson College into his diocese.

The archbishop was agreeable but sought to involve Father Henri Bellanger, a member of the Marist teaching order who had recently arrived at St. Michael's Church just up the road from the college. The priest turned out to be a stiff negotiator on behalf of his order, arranging for ownership of Jefferson College on favorable terms for the Marists. The archbishop was also able to convince the Federal occupiers to decamp and move upriver to White Hall Plantation. The shareholders were pleased, believing that they had ensured the future of their college.

St. Mary's Jefferson College

On July 1, 1864, twelve students and two émigré priests from France began the academic year at the newly renamed St. Mary's Jefferson College. The act of incorporation of the college for the Fathers of the Society of Mary can be found in the Marist archives in Atlanta—a document handwritten in elegant Spenserian script with flourishes and promises "to associate ourselves for a literary, scientific, religious and missionary purpose within the state of Louisiana." It acknowledged that the new owners took charge of an extensive campus, consisting of "the college building; two music rooms; alumni hall; math house; horse stable; carpenter shop; cow stable; servants house; kitchen and storeroom. Refectory; chapel; granary and infirmary; servants house; laundry; two carriages; two buggies; three carts; six horses; sixteen cows; and fifty swine."

In 1868, a Catholic newspaper lauded the new college as "rapidly becoming useful and permanent." Its curriculum offered ancient as well as modern languages, analytical construction and rhetoric, and "mathematics focused on mercantile transactions [though] higher classes have taken up the study of pure mathematics and physics." A bill from 1876 indicates that the cost for an enrolled student was $175.15 (the equivalent of approximately $3,700 in today's dollars), which covered tuition, room and board, "medical fees, washing, books and sundries, use of philosophical apparatus and chemicals, music lessons and use of musical instruments." A vintage photograph shows an impressive entrance to the campus with the porter's lodges flanking a dirt-track drive, hemmed by tall, dense hedges and wrapping around a lozenge-shaped garden filled with plantings and statuary.

Wandering journalist Martha Field, writing under the pseudonym Catherine Cole, visited St. Mary's in 1892 and found a small school of one hundred students, enrolled at both high school and college levels. Its band was "one of the best in the state," she wrote, and the boys' choir "[was] equal to any in an English cathedral." Valcour Aime's little chapel was "beautiful . . . with fine oak-raftered ceiling, handsome altar, and a very fine copy of Murillo's *Annunciation*."

In 1911, the Marists added the classical revival Science Hall that was completed in time for the college's golden jubilee celebrated two years later. That class was the largest graduating class in St. Mary's history—twenty-one young men. Yet St. Mary's, like its predecessors, had begun to totter financially, which provoked the order to augment tuition revenue by hosting an annual men's retreat. Even this proved insufficient to stanch their bleeding financial statement, however, and in July 1928, Fr. George Rapier, president of St. Mary's Jefferson College, received a letter from Rome. The vote to close the campus had been taken; St. Mary's Jefferson College was no more.

And, Finally, Manresa

An artist's rendering of the campus from the end of the Marists' tenure shows the grand Main Building surrounded by handsome two-story neoclassical buildings in a setting of trees and lawns. Listed for sale as "four tracts of land, all buildings and improvements, fixtures and machinery," the property aroused interest from several potential buyers, including one who proposed to open a convalescents' hospital. The winning bid, however, came from the Société Catholique D'Education Religieuse et Litteraire—the Order of the Society of Jesus, better known as the Jesuits. They agreed to pay $27,000 plus $500 cash for a property where they would continue the Marists' incipient project, namely, using the campus as a retreat facility.

The Society of Jesus already operated a retreat center in New Orleans, which they hoped to expand as well as separate its administration from other properties. College Point, though pleasantly isolated, was strategically located between the large Catholic populations of New Orleans and Baton Rouge and was quite accessible by automobile along the now-paved River Road.

The Jesuits renamed the campus "Manresa," for the Spanish cave where St. Ignatius of Loyola, founder of the order, made his first retreat and began formulating the Ignatian method of meditation. Manresa of St. James Parish would be an island of serenity amid the turmoil of everyday life, a place for reflection and spiritual rejuvenation for retreatants, ages eighteen to elderly. They were invited to spend several days searching for God and seeking peace, observing St. Ignatius's requirement of silence which, in 1931, no other retreat house in the United States maintained.

A 1937 article in a regional newspaper showed photographs of Manresa with rocking chairs by the library and a typical dormitory room located in the old Main Building. The bedroom was spartan, outfitted with an iron bed, plain wooden chair, and a throw rug on the old plank floor—clearly a place for spiritual exercise, not comfort.

When the retreat program began to prosper, the administration was faced with the decision of whether to renovate or tear down the Main Building. In what now seems like a fortuitous outcome, they failed to raise enough money for a new building and in 1947 began to renovate the old one. The renovation included added bedrooms and bathrooms, the installation of a sprinkler system and new roof, and refurbished common areas with new creature comforts.

Since then, what is now called St. Mary's Hall has again been refurbished. Valcour Aime's chapel, designated the Sacred Heart Chapel, was repaired and renovated after the discovery of termites; arcades were added between the chapel, Main Building, and a new dining hall, to shelter retreatants and staff in inclement weather. The porter's lodges were repaired, and a library was added in St. Mary's Hall. The President's House was renovated as additional housing for retreatants, and retreats were opened to include non-Catholic men. Manresa had become such a beloved institution that, during World War II, Rev. John Hynes reported letters received "from the western front, from the dripping jungles of Burma, from the wide reaches of the Pacific which say 'what I wouldn't give for three days at Manresa.'"

As I followed Tim Murphy through the grounds, it was evident that Manresa also nourishes a reverence for natural beauty. The main campus is enclosed on three sides by a dense forest; the hundred and fifty acres are elegantly landscaped and maintained by a dedicated grounds crew. Eight sprawling live oaks date from the Vavasseur plantation, and a double line of fourteen live oaks planted behind the Main Building in 1877 create a moss-draped, green tunnel. A dozen more live oaks from the same era shade the perimeter of the front lawn. Flower beds, camellia and satsuma trees, and sasanqua bushes adorn the campus. Walkways lined with azaleas wind past fountains and around ponds and religious statuary. Well-spaced lawn chairs dot the greenswards, and rocking chairs beckon from the galleries.

Across the River Road on open land is a spectacular allée of live oaks planted by an early president of St. Mary's. The property was leased as farmland into the 1970s but now is a favorite walk for retreatants who follow the allée to the levee, where a walking path on its crown offers commanding views of the river.

In one of the large rooms newly added to St. Mary's Hall, Manresa has lined a stack of bookshelves with a collection of albums that list the names of every retreat participant since the very first retreat took place in 1931. It furnishes an extraordinary record of the retreat history at Manresa.

As we studied them, I suddenly wished there was a similar record of the names, and even biographies, of the young men who had inhabited this place before—who had attended the College of Jefferson, Louisiana College, Jefferson College, and St. Mary's. It would be fitting, I thought, because their spirits, too, enliven and enrich this old plantation property long referred to as College Point.

II

Boats and the River

3
Pushin' Cargo

Tugboats pushing tows are iconic on the Mississippi River, I told Jeff Kindl. I've watched them slow-dance up and down the river for years and don't know anything about them because I live on the outside of the levees. So I'd like to ride along on a tugboat with barges to understand how they operate.

They're towboats, not tugboats, he politely corrected me. Jeff, as vice president of Gulf operations for American Commercial Barge Line, a marine transportation services company, is an authority on such things. Boats that push a rig of barges (up to fifty lashed together and called the "tow") have flat or squared bows so they can fit tightly against their load; tugboats have pointed bows. Tugs are used primarily to pull or nudge other vessels that can't move by themselves. In the Mississippi, they help a large or heavily loaded ship, such as an oceangoing freighter, to dock at a landing.

Perhaps my ignorance as a landlocked layperson amused Jeff because he agreed to arrange for me to spend a day on one of ACBL's vessels, where I would not only learn how to distinguish towboats from tugboats but also gain at least a superficial understanding of how these marine workhorses do their job. I'd be inside this world of metal and motors, within the fascinating parallel universe that operates along the inland waterway system, and between the levees on the lower Mississippi.

Towboats, also sometimes referred to as pusher craft, have plied this river for almost two centuries. Originally, steam-powered paddle wheelers moved rafts or barges lashed to their sides or pulled them along behind. When networks of railroads began to crisscross the country, much of the commerce moved off waterways and onto the more efficient rail systems. Increased trade returned to the river in the late 1930s after diesel-powered propeller boats were introduced. These new vessels, essentially floating engines, had the ability to push barges ahead of them, making the load more easily controlled and efficient. Today, towboats with their cargo-filled barges have an immense carrying capacity. According to the U.S. Army Corps of Engineers, a fifteen-barge tow can haul the equivalent of six locomotives pulling two hundred and sixteen railcars or more freight than one thousand eighteen-wheeler trucks lumbering along the nation's highways.

The river was a silvery ribbon of wave-cut water under a dawning sky streaked raspberry and lemon as the ACBL supply boat pulled up to the gently undulating main deck of the *Jacky L. O'Neal.* The *Jacky*'s white exterior practically glowed in the rising sun that seemed to spotlight her red-white-and-blue squared ACBL pennant logo. She was on a downriver trip from Cairo, Illinois, to Harahan, Louisiana, when we tied up alongside and I was instructed to clamber over the deck rail.

Towboats travel 24/7, Capt. Scott Richardson, the *Jacky*'s senior officer, told me when I sat with him later in the wheelhouse. So the Jacky wasn't going to pull ashore for me. Towboats are refueled and resupplied midstream while moving; specialty marine service boats pull alongside to deliver groceries, fuel, water, and any other necessities. "The only time we stop is for engine trouble or bad weather," he explained; "even in dense fog, we have to decide whether to continue on instruments or pull to the bank." It's an individual decision, depending on the size of the tow, condition of the river, and especially the captain's judgment and level of experience.

My adventure on the *Jacky* would take about ten hours, Jeff had forewarned me. Expect to ride most of the day, from embarking just above Port Allen to leaving the boat at Convent. This was only eighty river miles—not a long distance—and I had wondered how it could possibly take so long to cover a stretch I could drive in an hour and a half. But, as I learned onboard, a working towboat is the tortoise of the river. The *Jacky* was shepherding a tow of forty barges—an apron of metal spread out in front of her like a small park, eight across and five deep. In fact, if the collection of tightly fitted and lashed barges had been laid out across a cane field, it would have covered more than six acres.

With a load as large as this, forward progress can only be eight to ten miles per hour downriver at the best of times. And this calculates the sum of engine power plus a friendly current. When a loaded towboat travels upriver against the current, it is even slower—probably holding at only four or five miles per hour. This, despite the power of a towboat's engine, which, in the case of the *Jacky L. O'Neal*'s triple-screw engine, is a mind-boggling 9,120 horsepower.

Paul, a steersman, or apprentice mate learning the captain's trade, welcomed me aboard. Paul works twelve-hour shifts in order to learn towboating in both daytime and nighttime environments. He also inherits such menial tasks as orienting visitors to the boat, handing out the requisite pumpkin-orange life jackets, and offering safety briefings. These included warnings such as, "if you hear an alarm, come to the mess room" and "the overboard alarm is six short blasts."

The interior of the *Jacky* was freshly painted and did not show the expected wear of a well-used workboat. But this, as I later learned, was at least in part because she had been recently refurbished. She had been the *Harry M. Mack* until being overhauled, restored, and christened as the *Jacky L. O'Neal* a mere six months before. Her facelift had produced a clean-lined interior similar to an all-metal motel with her four decks connected by steep, narrow metal stairways as challenging as a gym's elliptical machine.

Paul's tour bypassed the extended, single-level stern deck that covered a hot, noisy engine room but led me through the foredecks. Because a towboat never stops, crew members remain on the boat during their rotations. They see nothing of the rest of the world lying a half mile to either side beyond the levees, never visiting a community, antebellum plantation, or historic church. It's a contained existence, almost as if motoring through a tunnel. Because of this, both work and leisure spaces are found within the *Jacky O'Neal*'s hull. Captain Scott condensed life on a towboat with the amusing, but apparently well-known epigram in towboating circles: "The only thing you have to look forward to is three hots and a cot"—meals and sleep time. Then, on his rotation every twenty-eight days, Captain Scott heads home for four weeks to his wife in Missouri.

On the *Jacky*'s first level, Paul showed me the galley and mess room (dining area); a rec room, equipped with satellite TV and Wi-Fi; a restroom; and the workshop for the boat's engineers. The second deck holds crew cabins and bathrooms as well as a mini-gym crammed with treadmills and other exercise equipment. Cabins and private bathrooms for the captain, pilot, and steersman as well as a guest room with en suite bath encompass the whole of the third deck. The guestroom looked inviting enough to make me regret I hadn't requested a longer voyage.

The fourth deck, the wheelhouse or pilothouse, is the *Jacky*'s command center. Much smaller in square footage than the other decks, it is windowed on all sides and, after having been raised nine feet in the boat's renovation, offers extraordinary views of the river's changing panorama. "We're about five stories in the air," Captain Scott told me as I peered out at the busy Mississippi sprawling around us. I saw other towboats with their loads, tugboats, and gargantuan freighters in the river, as well as docks and anchorages along the banks. I saw freighters and barges, some in parade formation, others in fleet positions, crowded near the battures. I watched Corps of Engineers dredges sucking up silt midriver and crews huddled on the banks repairing revetments and jetties.

The batture, the space between the water and the inside of the levee, was narrow in some spots, wide in others, crowded with marine industries and occasionally dense with trees and shrubs growing right to the water's edge. (These areas might be mistaken for parks, but there are no developed parks along the river below Baton Rouge.)

The wheelhouse also offers the only peek of the world beyond the levees: treetops, church steeples, and the metallic architecture of industry, with an occasional glimpse of a distant field or the roofs of a house or barn, the trim stack of a sugar mill.

"You're free to wander around," Paul had said hospitably, so I did, although I spent a disproportionate share of the day in the wheelhouse. I was captivated by the activities that engaged Captain Scott and Shane, the *Jacky*'s pilot, who spells the captain every six hours. Towboat pilots, I learned, are not the same as riverboat pilots. The latter, the Mark Twain variety, direct passage from a wheelhouse shared with a captain on oceangoing vessels on the Mississippi that ply the river between the Gulf of Mexico and Baton Rouge.

Shane as pilot is partway to earning his captain's stripes. He's outranked by Captain Scott but is in charge of the *Jacky* when he is on duty. He was focused and competent, but more tense than the captain who, after forty years on inland waterways, retains the unruffled manner of the droll airplane pilot who jokes over the intercom when the ride gets bumpy.

Their command center is a U-shaped console at the fore of the wheelhouse, arrayed with state-of-the-art navigational equipment. A battery of constantly changing computer screens above and below the laminate countertop attracted Captain Scott's attention as he simultaneously toyed with one of the two pairs of double, stainless-steel rods used to steer the boat and throttle the engines up or down. A color radar flashed dark green, reflecting the banks and present "obstacles"; a digitized, real-time map showed the locations of other boats on the river; a GPS screen indicated the *Jacky*'s position. The boat's speed and the speed of the current are visible on another screen, as was the depth of the water, which is monitored by depth finders positioned at the front corners of the load. I grew concerned after noticing that these often reported different readings at the same time; were we listing (the nautical term for "tilting")? No, the captain assured me. It meant that the river bottom was shallower toward the bank than midstream or that a towhead had changed the shape of the river bottom.

Among these sophisticated instruments, Captain Scott admitted that his favorite was still the marine radio. It is assuredly old-fashioned, but he believed that calling other boats on the dedicated channel, chatting with their wheelhouses, and listening to coast guard chatter were his most effective tools. "Twos," he said into the phone. This was river shorthand, left over from the days when captains used horns—toots—not telephones, to communicate with another boat about passing in opposite directions. "Twos" meant they would pass starboard to starboard. "Ones" meant they would pass port to port.

The wheelhouse phone's in-house channel connects all areas of the *Jacky O'Neal* to each other. When a whistle sound suddenly tweeted from the phone, the captain nodded and smiled. "That would be the engine room," he told me, lifting the receiver.

Helming a loaded towboat is a continuous challenge, with no autopilot. Soon after I came on board, we approached the Highway 190 bridge at Wilkerson Point and I was wary—actually worried—how a boat pushing forty barges could possibly pass through the bridge supports without scraping or hitting them. "If we could keep to the far right [span]," Captain Scott explained, "we could keep out of the current," which would make it easier to maneuver.

He was thinking out loud for my benefit, in his laconic manner, his words seeming to pass through his white, lampshade-shaped mustache. He manipulated his boat and tow into position and toggled the throttle; I could feel the revved-up vibrations and loud rumbles, and could tell by the speed at which we passed shrubs on the batture that we had slowed noticeably. Then we smoothly glided between two concrete support pillars with room to spare. And, since I was not in charge, I rewarded myself with a glance up as we passed under a bridge I'd crossed many times. Its undergirding of industrial grade metal resembled lacework, while the strips of divided highway looked like two textured ribbons.

From Baton Rouge to New Orleans is the most congested segment of the fourth longest river in the world; it teems with continuous traffic. Heading downstream gave the *Jacky* the advantage of having right of way, but we slowed down around bends because "the water is faster on the bend side, rather than the point side," Captain Scott said, although he tried to remain in the channel wherever possible because of the size of his load. At Conrad Point I heard his casual tone shift into a growl: an upriver-bound towboat with a small load was clearly in our way and going too slowly to avoid us on the present course. Clearly peeved, Captain Scott changed our vector and mumbled about how the other captain had disregarded both the regulations and accustomed protocols of the river.

Further downriver, he pointed out a dark line in the water, bold enough for even my inexperienced eye to see. It might have been a reef, a trailing end of a known (and slightly visible) sandbar, but he had to quickly decide where to steer the *Jacky* because the water might be shallow. Conversely, the dark line might signal a deep water break. The captain monitored the depth readers, then growled again slightly and built up speed to keep the boat and load from sliding sideways toward the bank. As we passed to the starboard side, I spied a flat bed of sand peeking out of the water, a sandbar, on which a small blue heron perched. The heron, unlike my captain, was delighted with the mid-stream formation that allowed him to peruse the water for prey.

The wheelhouse also offered the best perspective of our tow, which resembled parallel lines of gridlocked boxcars in a haphazard arrangement of colors—mustard yellow, forest green, white, dove gray, sand colored, and rust brick. I asked what the colors indicated. "Nothing in particular," I was told.

A typical container barge is thirty-five feet wide by two hundred feet long, a bit larger than a double-wide trailer. Heretofore, I'd assumed that barges were uniformly built, but in fact, their shapes can differ. Most are the stereotypical shoebox rectangles with four straight sides, but some are rectangular with a sloped end, called a bow or rake, similar to the prow of other boats. These barges are always positioned at the head or rear of a tow, to take advantage of the way a sloped edge moves more efficiently through water, lessening the drag, whether the pusher craft is going forward or in reverse. Barges also have different drafts.

Barge design varies according to what loads they carry. Hopper barges are open and carry coal, iron, sand—cargo that won't be damaged by getting wet. Covered barges are specifically constructed to keep cargo dry and, in the case of certain products like wheat and corn, protected from blowing away. Some covered barges are designated for dry cargo; others carry only "wet" cargo such as oil and chemicals. Barge covers are ridged fiberglass, with hatches that are used for both loading cargo and allowing cleaners inside to decontaminate the hold between loads. The area below the cargo hold is sectioned off, a safety mechanism to prevent water that accidentally enters from saturating the contents. Every barge also has an individual identification, a stenciled combination of letters and numbers that are entered on the trip's manifest. This document also lists the content of each barge and other relevant information.

The arrangement of barges in a tow is both art and science and is determined by whether a barge is full or empty and by where it will be delivered if the entire tow does not terminate at the same place. Gerald, the *Jacky*'s lead deckhand, told me he had worked on a lot of rivers for thirty years. Rigging the tow must make it seamless, he emphasized in describing his work. If not, the load can become dangerous. Barges escaping their tows have often made the local news along the River Road, causing wrecks on the river or ramming into bridge pilings.

The *Jacky*'s four deckhands are charged with wiring up the tow as well as releasing barges delivered before the terminal stop. Making the *Jacky*'s tow had required connecting the forty barges, one to another, with numerous lines, or ropes. Each of these, some synthetic, some metal, has a different name and is connected to and with a militia of hardware. There are wires and ratchets, winches, shackles, pins, links, and straps.

The rear barges abutting the towboat were also connected on both port and starboard sides with five thick lines to prevent the barges from sliding or bumping into each other or the towboat. Every couple of days, the deck crew must check each connection—at the oblong cleats, the cylindrical cleats, the short round ones, the cleats painted school-bus yellow—to make sure they're holding as tight as when the trip began. Additionally, the deck crew is responsible for maintaining the boat, both inside and out, when they are not checking the tow.

I went below with Captain Scott for the second seating of lunch, following Shane and the other crew members on for the next six-hour shift. We gathered around the mess-hall table large enough for eight, part of the large galley that is the domain of the cheerful, grandmotherly Doris. She had traded a longtime job in a nursing home two years ago to cook for the *Jacky*'s crew. Doris's rotation is twenty-one days afloat, twenty-one days off, when she returns to her husband in Tennessee.

The *Jacky*'s new stainless steel galley is equipped and serviceable enough for a decent-sized commercial restaurant. Her pantry shelves are well stocked, and two refrigerator/freezers are packed as tightly as the tow load because Doris feeds the ten-man crew three full meals each day. She starts each day at 3:00 a.m., she told me, to cook and serve a full breakfast from 5:00 to 6:00 a.m. She cleans up, then starts on lunch for the two working shifts, serving from 11:00 to noon. She cleans up again, then produces dinner, served from 5:00 to 6:00 p.m. On the day I joined them, the *Jacky*'s crew selected from a cafeteria-style lunch of fried and broiled fish, fried shrimp, hushpuppies, French fries, dirty rice, an extensive salad bar including fruit and cole slaw, and three choices for dessert. "I go to bed early every night," Doris confided.

She can rely on a few planned templates such as taco Tuesday, Friday fish fry, and Sunday night pizza. Otherwise, she must create every menu, factoring in what she likes to cook with the crew's favorites dishes. After she plans the meals, she emails her order for foodstuffs and necessities to whichever marine store will be closest to make the delivery. Some meals are made mostly from scratch and some use a variety of culinary shortcuts, such as readymade pie crusts. Doris and the other female cook who spells her are the only women in the crew, but they appear to have developed an easy comradery with the guys.

Jeff Kindl had predicted that the highlight of my day afloat would be the opportunity to walk out the length of the thousand-foot-long tow to its head. In mid-afternoon, I donned my orange life vest and followed three members of the deck crew across the *Jacky*'s bow deck. For the first time, I noticed two double, forward-facing staircases that rise high above her deck. Tow knees, my escorts told me, used when the load is empty and barges float higher, allowing the boat to adjust to their level.

We threaded our way past a tangle of lines and into the center of the tow, a procession of agile feet, sidestepping assorted cleats, tiptoeing over the ropes that crisscrossed at each barge corner, balancing on the narrow rims of the barge decks. If I glanced down, I could usually see a glistening sliver of water just beneath us, through the narrow crack where the barges didn't quite touch.

And then we reached the head of the tow. The river, whipped by the wind, sloshed over the barge decks and I stood there, right at the level of the water, midstream in the Mississippi River, balancing against the hold wall of the lead barge and rocking with the undulations of the river. As I held tight, I surveyed the broad and immediate vista of the river sprawled before me. It was as if I were on a slow-moving, metal beach and had achieved, however briefly, the feeling that I was part of the river.

It was almost five o'clock when the *Jacky O'Neal* approached the small community of Convent. A tugboat from ACBL's facility there pulled alongside to ferry me ashore, and the two boats rocked in synchrony as I climbed over the *Jacky*'s railing, then settled into the tug's dark interior for the speedy ride to the landing. As I began to climb the levee, not quite ready to return to life on the other side, I could swear that I heard the *Jacky* giving me a farewell toot . . . but perhaps it may only have been her signal to another boat that they would be passing each other port to port.

4
Lock It Up

You may have wondered about a small, dapper-looking Cape Dutch–style building perched on a rise in downtown Plaquemine near the Mississippi River. With a slick white-brick exterior, a dark, pitched roof with stepped gable ends, and trim of chocolate brown, it looks a bit out of place among its mostly classical revival, Queen Anne revival, and turn-of-the-century commercial-style neighbors. But the Gary James Hebert Memorial Lockhouse is not a misfit in this old river town; it has stood guard at the once-important convergence of Bayou Plaquemine and the river for over a century.

In the heyday of the lockhouse during the first half of the twentieth century, the jaunty little building held the brains and brawn of the old Plaquemine Lock, a "water elevator" that connected the bayou and the river. The old lock itself is still visible just beyond the lockhouse windows. It's an open concrete chamber that extends from the slope of the Mississippi River levee to the bayou beyond and seems much too narrow for anything larger than a motorboat or a small yacht. Yet its iron gates admitted more than a thousand boats of all kinds each year, including commercial packets and towboats pushing barges. The little lock played an important role in Mississippi River navigation during a certain part of Louisiana's history. And the little lockhouse is a three-room museum filled with antiques and artifacts, photos, and equipment relating to its days of purpose, including a working model of the old lock, just to show visitors what a boat passage would have been like.

It is fortunate that the lockhouse and lock are still here because, after they had been decommissioned, they were slated for demolition. The nearby highway needed to be widened. Only a four-year battle, led by the eponymous Mr. Hebert, saved the lock and its campus. They were too significant in Plaquemine's history to be lost, he declared. So they weren't, which was why the little building was named in his honor.

The odd name "Plaquemine" was given to both bayou and town, derived from the French colonists' interpretation of an Attakapas Indian word for persimmon, "Piakemines." Iberville had documented the existence of the bayou in his 1699 journal, noting it was choked with river debris. But French settlers in the early eighteenth century learned from local Native Americans that Bayou Plaquemine was quite navigable during Mississippi River high water. The bayou wound west, connecting with a network of streams into the Atchafalaya Basin, which gave the confluence great potential for transportation and commerce, an obvious place for a settlement. In 1838, the town of Plaquemine was formally established, and by the time the lock was built in the early twentieth century, the community had become a busy hub for the cypress lumber industry.

Early residents of Plaquemine had not anticipated living with the Mississippi River's annual flooding, however, so when high water filled the bayou, an outcry for flood control arose. In 1867, Iberville Parish constructed a levee at the head of the bayou with a dirt road across its crown. Wagons could then cross the bayou, but boats were forced to seek alternate routes to the river. This was still the era when the most reliable transportation in rural south Louisiana was by boat, not overland, so although the levee had mitigated flooding, it had also impeded commerce. What else could be done?

The solution was to build a lock. Such a structure would control water entering the bayou from the river, which pleased those concerned about flooding; it would also allow a connection between the bayou and the river, which pleased those with commercial interests. Furthermore, a lock might improve the hydrology of the bayou by reducing its annual clogging and silting and the subsequent need to dredge in order to maintain a navigable channel.

Consideration of a lock percolated for a decade until, eventually, all government entities—the town of Plaquemine, parish of Iberville, and state of Louisiana—unified to petition Congress. A lock at the confluence of Bayou Plaquemine and the Mississippi River would be in the national interest, they no doubt argued, and would benefit commerce on the river. Surprisingly, the federal government agreed.

After fourteen years, the bankruptcies of several contractors, and unexpected, and expensive, remedies for the alarming discovery that the river end of the lock was mired in quicksand, Plaquemine's new engineering marvel was finally completed. The first boat to pass through the $1.3 million project on the red-letter day of March 13, 1909, was a government vessel, the *Stadia*.

The Plaquemine Lock had been designed by Col. George W. Goethals, assistant to the chief engineer of the Army Corps of Engineers. Goethals is credited with introducing high-lift locks to domestic civil engineering; the lock at Bayou Plaquemine, with a lift of fifty-one feet, became the highest freshwater lift in the world at that time. It could also have been spotlighted as the only hydraulically operated river lock system in the United States.

The lock chamber measured 547 feet long and 55 feet wide, a

long rectangle with thick concrete walls enclosed by two redundant sets of hinged gates at each end. All four operated independently. Goethals also designed the two-story lockhouse, more accurately defined as the Power House because it contained the machinery that operated the gates. Local lore suggested that Colonel Goethals chose the Dutch Cape architectural style because he was Dutch, but the engineer had been born in Brooklyn. It had also been surmised that the use of glazed white brick on the exterior was to protect the building from the steam produced inside and was reflective so that searchlights from boats approaching in the dark could tell where the lock was.

Although the Plaquemine Lock was important to Mississippi River navigation in the early twentieth century, it barely registered as a footnote on George Goethals's résumé. Five years later, he gained international recognition as chief engineer for the Panama Canal, which eclipsed any fame that might have accrued to him from the little lock at Plaquemine.

Today, part of the lockhouse museum is dedicated to an exhibit of Goethals's engineering, for the sake of visitors like me who are not knowledgeable about lock operations. Goethals's design incorporated boilers to create steam which ran water pumps. In the late 1940s, electric motors replaced the steam equipment; thereafter, the push of a button could create the water pressure required to operate the gates, an upgrade that put the two lockmen out of a job. They had previously been required to enter tunnels behind the lock walls to adjust the steam valves. Today, two circular windows, appearing decorative in scale and design, are visible at the bayou end of the lockhouse; they are actually relic openings of the old boilers.

The parts of the lock visible to the public were the chamber and the two sets of steel gates. Those at the Mississippi River entrance were reinforced with riveted iron plates to counter the river's immense current and, like the bayou-end gates, had been planned for redundancy in case of malfunction. But the two sets of gates also offered the advantage of efficiency when a small boat came through. Then, only the internal set of gates was used, reducing the amount of water filling the chamber and the time to do so.

When a vessel was calmed within the chamber, deckhands or crew members secured the boats and barges to sturdy iron hitches in the chamber walls as the water level changed. These weathered holds still remain, visible within darkened niches on the lock walls.

Locals of a certain age remember crossing a walkway on the top of the bayou-end gates when the lock was idle. This offered a more convenient way across the bayou than going out to the highway. When the lock was in use, however, no one was allowed on the gates, so patrolling the locks became one of the lockmaster's consistent duties.

Packets, fishing vessels, houseboats, towboats with barges, and other watercraft passed through the Plaquemine Lock. Commercial boats carrying lumber, sugar, cotton, and petroleum products could arrive any time of day or night, which was one of the reasons that the lockmaster and his assistant lived on the grounds. According to Richard Trepagnier, son of an assistant lockmaster, when a vessel approached the lock, it tooted its horn three times. The lockhouse responded in kind. When the water inside the lock had leveled and the boat could be permitted to exit, the lockhouse blew a single whistle to announce the gate opening. Richard, an active member of the nonprofit support group Friends of the Plaquemine Lock, sounded nostalgic recalling the toots and whistles of yesteryear that disappeared with the introduction of marine radios.

Boats that approached the lock from the Mississippi often had to tie up at a guide wall to await entry. Towboats with barges would moor at this line of creosoted timbers on the upriver side of the entry and, riding the powerful current, often rammed the posts hard enough to cause damage. This offered young men like himself summer jobs repairing the posts, Richard recalled.

The Plaquemine Lock Historic Site is "a park where you can

still find people who remember it as it was in its heyday," said Stan Richardson. He is the director here and believes that contributions from Richard and others like him help bring the story of the lock alive for visitors.

The average duration of a boat's passage through the lock was about an hour, but towboats with tows, especially ones entering from the bayou, could take much longer. The bayou end was a more challenging approach due to a bend and two bridges only a short distance from the gates. Occasionally barges were simply pulled on ropes down the bayou and into the lock, and when a tow consisted of many barges, its passage might take two or three days since the lock could only hold one barge at a time. Furthermore, one old-timer wryly noted, if a large barge entered the lock with two coats of paint, it would have lost one by the time it came out the other end.

The Plaquemine Lock served the area well until after World War II, when larger boats were built and river traffic increased. A new lock was needed. The Port Allen Lock, constructed about ten miles upriver, opened in 1961, offering much greater chamber capacity plus direct connections with both the river and the Intracoastal Waterway. And its accesses were easy—no bends or bridges to impede traffic, and little chance of scraped paint.

When the new lock opened, the Plaquemine Lock officially closed, becoming something of a white elephant for the Corps of Engineers. Their last construction project at the site was to rebuild a levee across the river entrance of the lock, to provide, in Corps vernacular, "continued integrity to the Mississippi River levee flood protection system." The now-continuous levee furnished assurance that the only way a boat could travel from the river into Bayou Plaquemine was to portage over a twenty-foot-high dike.

In 1969, Gary Hebert editorialized about the condition of the lock property, describing the nineteen-acre campus as "like a ghost town." In the eight years since the lock had been decommissioned, he had watched it become seedy and overgrown, the great iron gates rusting. Most of the outbuildings were gone. The lockmaster's house had been sold and moved to a residential lot on Highway 1; a warehouse used for storing tools and machinery had been demolished for its lumber; a second warehouse and the home of the assistant lockmaster had been bought by a local business and moved into town; the boathouse overlooking the bayou had been demolished.

The newspaper publisher thought the property was a historic asset for Plaquemine and Louisiana and should be saved. However, the Louisiana Department of Highways disagreed. In 1972 they announced plans to widen nearby LA 1 to four lanes, expropriating a swathe of lock property and filling in the lock and part of the bayou. Frustrated Plaquemine drivers approved.

Gary Hebert, however, grew increasingly resolute about saving this valuable part of Plaquemine's history. He crusaded, encouraging the state's Office of Historic Preservation to place it on the National Register of Historic Places. The designation, though conferring no legal status for preservation, made a statement of principle. The lock was added to the National Register.

Area residents, adamant about fixing the traffic problem, directed their anger at the man trying to thwart "progress." "He made enemies," his widow Joyce Hebert told a reporter years later. "My children were taunted at school." Readers canceled subscriptions to the newspaper and some advertisers took their business elsewhere. "We were like outcasts for a little while," she recalled.

Then, somehow, the Highway Department figured out a way to build the new four-lane approach without encroaching on the lock property. The road expansion, completed to cheers in 1979, was completely clear of the lock and lockhouse. And eventually, Joyce Hebert reported with evident satisfaction, most of her husband's opponents began to realize the significance of his efforts.

The long ordeal concluded happily when the property was transferred to the state of Louisiana in 1999 and made a state historic site. The lockhouse was transformed into a museum open to the public and named for its champion. The grounds became part of the exhibit space. One of the old gates remains on site—an ironwork the faded black color of an old cast-iron cooking pot and as massive as a fortress wall. Another artifact on the grounds is a tan concrete, ramped structure with a broad niche in its midsection. This is the framework from which one set of gates had hung.

Across the site, at the former location of the old lockmaster's house, stands a pavilion housing a collection of Atchafalaya Basin workboats dating from the first half of the twentieth century. These authentic pirogues, bateaux, Lafitte skiffs, and even a houseboat that operated as a floating store in the swamp "all have a story to tell," Stan Richardson said. And most of them might have passed through the old Plaquemine Lock on a regular basis.

One of the least appreciated elements of the Plaquemine Lock State Historic Site is its river overlook, which affords one of the most accessible and dramatic views of the river anywhere along the River Road. From this elevated vantage point, a visitor sees a broad reach of water downriver, and the sharp elbow of Plaquemine Point folding upriver. I never miss the opportunity to enjoy this view but often leave somewhat amused, realizing that none of the large vessels I can see on the river could possibly squeeze through the old and historic Plaquemine Lock.

5
The Bridge to Nowhere

If you squint and tilt your head just right on the east-bank approach to the Sunshine Bridge, the erector-set construction in the distance can look a bit like the metal skeleton of a dinosaur rising above the cane fields. Its two towers resemble the bony plates of the ancient beast's back; the soot-gray access road peels down, resembling its neck, and I can imagine its unseen head buried in the rustling green fields of sugarcane that still sprawl across the landscape. With blinders on to limit your view, to exclude the metal sculptures of nearby petrochemical plants, this perspective might be quite similar to how this scene appeared in 1964 when the $30 million project was completed. It proudly spanned the river, from cane fields on the east bank to cane fields on the west bank, and was fondly dubbed "the Bridge to Nowhere." It was a splendid example of the adage, "if you build it, they will come . . . eventually."

The Sunshine Bridge was the first bridge constructed across the Mississippi River between New Orleans and Baton Rouge in this region so historically dependent on ferries. But the offices for economic development in the respective local parishes, as well as those at state-government level, wanted to lure more petrochemical industries to the area. Success would necessitate an easy river crossing—"a fixed, all-weather crossing," in the lingo of the Louisiana Department of Highways. That meant a bridge instead of ferries whose service was impaired by bad weather or boat or engine problems. (This reasoning naturally ignored potential delays and closures of the "fixed crossing" as might happen when an accident occurred atop or a barge slammed into the bridge pilings.)

Few seemed to remember that an earlier version of a Mississippi River bridge between New Orleans and Baton Rouge had already been envisioned. In the early 1950s during Governor Earl Long's term, an eighty-mile toll road from Gramercy to Lafayette had been proposed. The Acadian Thruway would connect with the Airline Highway in the Lutcher/Gramercy area and offer an alternate to old Highway 90 from New Orleans to Acadiana. It would include a bridge that would cross the river near Gramercy. This route, however, completely bypassed Baton Rouge and was scrapped, although its detour from the state capital wasn't given as a reason. Rather, they said, it was because the Federal-Aid Highway Act of 1956 (known as the National Interstate and Defense Highways Act) had funded what would become Interstate 10, creating a direct road from New Orleans to the west, and passing right through Baton Rouge.

The idea for a bridge along the River Road between New Orleans and Baton Rouge steeped for almost a decade until, according to local lore, a state representative from Ascension Parish buttonholed Governor Jimmie Davis to say that a bridge built in his parish would boost economic development significantly. And, as added incentive, the legislator proposed that the bridge could be named for Mr. Davis. Perhaps it was only circumstantial then that Jimmie Davis happened to create the Ascension–St. James Bridge and Ferry Authority in 1960, and charged it with oversight of construction of a bridge located within parts of the named parishes. Furthermore, this bridge, also coincidentally, became known as the Sunshine Bridge. Davis, a country singer before becoming governor, had demurred at having the bridge named for him; neither was it named in honor of his hit recording "You Are My Sunshine," he protested, nor in honor of his horse, Sunshine. The name of the bridge was chosen simply because it would have an east-west alignment, just like the sun.

The ASJBF Authority was chaired by a Donaldsonville dentist, who met monthly with three other appointed businessmen to discuss planning for the bridge. These confabs were held wherever convenient as the Authority had no offices; occasionally, the venue was the Hotel Donaldson in which the chair was known to be an investor. (He later sold his holdings when it became a distraction to the Authority's credibility.)

The Authority was charged with overseeing construction and operation of a four-lane toll bridge with three toll booths and room for their expansion. This required securing rights of way and land for a west-bank toll plaza as well as land for access roads on both sides of the river. As it was drawn, the bridge would be located seven miles downriver from Donaldsonville on the west bank; on the east bank, it landed near no particular community.

Bonds, "not financed by taxpayers," would underwrite the project, the Authority members boasted, although the state (i.e., dollars from taxpayers) would be financially responsible should the Authority be unable to service the bond payments. The revenue source would be bridge tolls, projected in the 1961 prospectus to be $1.5 million annually by 1972. (The actual amount was only slightly more than $.5 million.)

Nevertheless, optimism prevailed at the outset and, in October 1961, construction contracts were let. One contract for $20.3 million covered the substructure; this was over budget. The other, for the superstructure, came in lower than its estimate. An additional $10 million was required for land acquisition and building approaches and toll plaza. But since connector roads from the approaches to main highways on each side were beyond the scope of this project, both ends of the bridge landed "nowhere," in the sweeps of sugarcane planted on both sides of the river.

Construction of the Sunshine Bridge began in August 1962. It was to be a standard double-cantilever, a design first used in 1867 in Germany. Its strength and stability crossing the river were ensured by horizontal projections supported by continuous steel trusses through the deck. The bridge's main span of 825 feet plus its suspended spans of 800 feet on each side meant that the length of the bridge tallied almost a mile and three quarters. Seven piers on pilings were sunk as deep as eighty feet into the riverbed to support the gargantuan structure and its four-lane roadway. (The complicated engineering required to sink pilings in the Mississippi River is another story unto itself.) The undercarriage of the bridge measured 133 feet, designed to allow clearance no matter how high the water. In an aerial photograph of the just-completed bridge taken in 1964, the structure is a graceful arch capped with silvery latticework peaks, resting on pylons that disappear into a tranquil stream. It is a regal span across the mighty river.

This being Louisiana, it was not surprising that the ASJBF Authority was the focus of some political scandal. Allegations of inflated salaries and payment to an oil company not to drill on a bridge right-of-way created stories in the press. A further stench arose when it was revealed that legal and engineering fees paid for the Sunshine Bridge were greater than those paid for the new Greater New Orleans Bridge, even though the latter was a larger project. Most intriguing was the charge that the engineering firm for the Sunshine Bridge had been paid for a plan they had simply "dusted off"—the plan for the never-built Acadian Thruway bridge, which they were accused of passing off as original for Jimmie Davis's project. "The Authority needs to prove it is not wasting taxpayer money," a local newspaper editorial growled.

Incoming governor John McKeithen had relished the gossip and successfully ran on a pledge to clean up politics, including to "rid the state of the Sunshine Bridge gang."

Despite suspicions and snarls, the Sunshine Bridge opened on October 12, 1964, twenty-nine months after construction began, and a month early. The daughter of the state senator who had introduced the bill creating the bridge authority cut the ribbon at the gleaming, new west-bank toll plaza. She was surrounded by representatives of the engineering and construction firms, a sampling of politicians, three clergy offering blessings, several high school bands, and a large group of excited local residents who were as thrilled by the dependable "fixed all-weather crossing" as was the economic development crowd. A celebratory motorcade—considered a real parade—drove across the new bridge deck to the east bank, then returned to the toll plaza, to a barbecue lunch open to the public. The director of state highways said, to applause, that "the bridge would have a very positive impact on the industrialization of the area and the state." Two days later, it had a positive impact on west-bank LSU football fans whose shorter journey—in both time and distance—to Tiger Stadium had alleviated the worry of missing the kickoff because of a poorly timed ferry.

The beautiful new bridge served the area well, collecting tolls and facilitating river crossing, but it still stood, looking misplaced and forgotten, amongst waving rows of sugarcane. Soon enough, the lack of linkage to other highways began to aggravate regular commuters, even as many had been pleased to adopt the convenience (and discounted pricing) of ticket books. They also found it irritating that the number of exemptions from paying tolls was so broad; national guardsmen in uniform, ambulances, school buses, deputy sheriffs, even haulers of sugarcane were favored. Their complaints rose until Governor McKeithen removed the unpopular tolls for everyone. Soon, however, they were reinstated; then they were removed again. It was sometimes difficult, locals recalled, to know whether tolls were on or off.

For four years, the Sunshine Bridge was a looming and prominent presence, industrially handsome, offering swift passage across the river, only to terminate at the narrow, winding River Road on each bank. "Maybe the bridge was built a little ahead of its time," one politician observed, as new industries were built (as predicted) and burgeoning traffic, including eighteen-wheelers, clogged the narrow roadways.

"Traffic suffers undue burdens," said another local politician, claiming access to the bridge was "as outdated as paddle wheelers."

Finally, in 1968, relief arrived on the east bank, where numerous industrial plants had been completed. A two-lane connector road, LA 22, linked the bridge to the new interstate highway in Sorrento, although the comparable west bank link was not completed until 1973.

That was the same year that the Authority formally relinquished control of the bridge to the Louisiana Department of Highways, transferring the bond obligations of the bridge to the state. This included debt on the bonds issued to build the bridge, contrary to the bridge authority's original promise. Although tolls, when collected, had been dedicated to operation and maintenance of the bridge as well as to bond obligations, they had never raised sufficient funding to pay the interest. So the Highway Department inherited regular payments and interest plus the payrolls and benefits for the dedicated bridge personnel. Despite the need for funding, however, in 1979 the legislature voted to remove the tolls, a politically popular but fiscally shortsighted decision. They offered no substitute for the million or so dollars that the sixty-cent toll generated annually.

When the tolls were removed, the empty toll plazas and a small utility building nearby began to suffer from lack of maintenance, becoming eyesores and attracting vandals. Yet they remained as decorative fixtures on the bridge approach until, inevitably, a man accidentally crashed his car into the toll booth in 1984. Four years later, a delivery truck clipped the canopy, resulting in the driver's death. And then, although tolls were not being collected, the toll booths were rebuilt. This proved a prescient decision as the following year one-dollar tolls were reinstated, yielding over $2 million annually for the state, and a storm of complaints. The tolls were soon reduced, then removed.

Through the years, the state has been required to repair and update the bridge numerous times, as befits a structure that is now over fifty years old and used by more than 22,000 vehicles daily. Cleaning and repainting rusting girders and beams, resurfacing the pocked roadway, upgrading lighting, and a roster of other maintenance duties have fallen under the purview of the Highway Department, without the benefit of dedicated funding, aka tolls.

In 2013, a state senator suggested that he might propose legislation to bring back tolls in order to help offset the costs of bridge maintenance. Revenue would be twice as much as it had been in the 1990s, he projected, if a fifty-cent toll was collected on each side (not just on the west-bank approach). This could generate slightly more than $4 million annually. When political leaders from the River Parishes offered a roster of considerations to be added to his proposal in exchange for their support, the idea of reinstating tolls on the Sunshine Bridge vanished.

But the Bridge to Nowhere remained, a vital link from Somewhere to Somewhere for a much-expanded petrochemical industry and for residents wanting to cross the wide Mississippi. It remains part of the area's hurricane evacuation plan as well.

Today, the Sunshine Bridge is no longer the only fixed, all-weather crossing between New Orleans and Baton Rouge; two more have subsequently been added. But the old bridge still garners some of the same excitement it generated when it unceremoniously dumped travelers into the cane fields.

Perhaps the east-west orientation at certain times of day has added to its charm, just as Jimmie Davis said. It's an attribute one Facebook user extolled in a gushing post: "I love going over this bridge when the sun is setting," she wrote; "it's amazingly awesome." Which may be the best compliment possible for a piece of middle-aged infrastructure with something of a checkered history.

6

The River Angel and His Ritz

If I hadn't signed up for a day of paddling on the Mississippi River a couple of years ago, I would never have discovered Poche Park in Paulina and met its cheery and eponymous owner, Charlie Poche.

That is because the park is a campground that is both inaccessible and invisible to people who drive the River Road. It is available solely for those adventurers who explore the river by boat—in a canoe, a rowboat, even a raft. They may be through paddlers—journeying the twenty-three hundred miles from the headwaters of the river at Lake Itasca, Minnesota, all the way to the Gulf of Mexico—or travelers, like those on the Quapaw Canoe Company adventure I joined, whose journey covers only a limited segment of the river. All of them are welcome at Charlie's place.

It was serendipity that I'd learned about John Ruskey's guided canoe trip from Baton Rouge to the Gulf. John, a dedicated outdoorsman, has plied the Mississippi for twenty-five years and has turned his passion into a business: Quawpaw, based in Clarksdale, Mississippi, offers guided river trips of varying lengths and experience levels and creates educational programming about the river for all age groups. John's mission is specifically to promote a greater appreciation for "the magnificent beauty and wonders of the Lower Mississippi River and its Floodplain Valley."

One of his contributions is to have mapped the lower river for the benefit of small-boat travelers, compiling a complete, mile-by-mile guide to the river from St. Louis to the Gulf. Rivergator, as he calls the digital encyclopedia, records and annotates everything along the river, including sites of interest; dangers to small boaters such as ferry crossings and a wastewater outfall from a chemical plant; topographical attractions such as sandbars, wetlands, and beaches suitable for a daytime stop or for camping overnight. Like Poche Park.

Such sites are common along the upper and middle reaches of the river, where travelers can find numerous wild and hospitable-looking banks available at quitting time. But they are hard to come by below Baton Rouge, where the river banks are well developed and crammed cheek-to-jowl with "a mix of dry-docks, granaries, shipyards, scrapyards, fertilizer plants, petro-chemical plants, stevedores, container docks, resupply docks, and everything else imaginable to serve the commerce needs of America's interior," as John has described them. Because of this, Poche Park has come to be considered a riverside Ritz Carlton, a welcome anomaly on the "business end" of the river. And Charlie Poche is the only Cajun "river angel" along the length of the big river, as the small-boat river travelers call the assortment of altruists who live along the river and offer help in a variety of ways.

When I first contacted John Ruskey, a crew of eight had signed up for his two-week paddle, but he graciously agreed to let me join them for a day of my choosing. That turned out to be the twenty-mile segment from the Sunshine Bridge down to Paulina and their campsite at Poche Park.

John's crew and their gear were packed into two large Voyageur canoes when I eased myself into the second seat of the larger canoe and hefted the paddle. We were in the west-bank shadow of the bridge and began to cross the busy channel, wary of a fast-moving tugboat and an oceangoing freighter that rode high and cast a huge, sloshing wake. Thereafter, we paddled close to the east bank, occasionally sliding through the shadow of a moored freighter that loomed overhead, its deckhands far above us hollering down at the unusual sight of canoes in their river.

A steady headwind and intermittent rain squalls made progress seem slow, so it was late afternoon when I spied the large white sign by a stand of willows that read "Welcome paddlers, mile marker 149, Paulina, LA." The mile reference meant that the campground was one hundred and forty-nine river miles above Head of Passes, the bird's foot river delta at the Gulf of Mexico, which is how people on the river measure distances.

As we pulled ashore, we were greeted by an older man, his white hair ruffling in the wind, a broad smile on his face. It was Charlie. As I glanced about the campground, I saw a wide, undeveloped swathe of tan-colored sand, dotted with dense stands of willows. A few dunes and ridges and water cuts added interest to the setting; later I learned that the natural cove on the downriver side of the campground is home to alligators, beaver, and other wildlife, but they didn't appear then.

But, I learned from the paddlers, it's the amenities that Charlie provides that have earned Poche Park kudos from river travelers. He had hospitably stacked firewood near a readymade fire bowl and installed a hand pump that delivers gushes of nonpotable water from a faucet, complete with drain, for washing dishes and muddy feet. He had positioned a square metal table with four chairs in the shade of a stand of willows, augmenting this seating arrangement with several long beams set strategically nearby.

Three flagpoles flew banners that reflected his allegiances: an American flag, a Louisiana flag, and the black-and-white skull and crossbones of pirates. Other tall poles that he installed supported automatic solar lights and lights rigged to a portable generator, to illuminate the camp after dark. Paddlers are always invited to pitch tents or camp "anywhere they want," Charlie offered hospitably.

Once upon a time, Charlie told me, he had positioned a portable toilet onsite, but one of the river's high-water events had washed it away. A flood also claimed a decorative picket fence he had pounded into the sand to outline the camp's perimeter and also took additional beams in the sitting area, and a variety of miscellaneous decorations. He knows very well that the river gives, and the river takes.

The campsite and its amenities all come free of charge, as do the occasional use of his home washer and dryer or a lift to a nearby store for provisions.

Jordan Hanssen is another great fan of Poche Park. Jordan's Seattle-based nonprofit, OAR Northwest, is an environmental education program that brings college students down the river in rowboats, capturing water samples that are sent back to a lab for microbe analysis. His crews also visit at local schools to talk about the Mississippi River. Jordan first learned of Poche Park in 2014 by consulting a community website for Mississippi River travelers and has visited the campground several times.

"The upper Mississippi is much more conducive to people in small boats," he told me, echoing John Ruskey. "Other than this," Jordan reiterated, "campsites between Baton Rouge and New Orleans are just places to pull over between industrial sites. And [finding them] depends on the river level."

I abandoned Poche Park, my fellow canoeists, and our host to go home and learned a few days later that the Quapaw paddlers had been forced to evacuate the campground after the incessant rain became torrential. Their refuge was transformed into a flat. They left by support vans until the rain ceased the following day.

That weather, Charlie told me later with regret, exposed his campground's greatest flaw: the beach is really "just a thin surface layer of sand over Mississippi mud." It always turns sludgy in heavy rains. He's hoping that, with luck, the river's errant flow will gift him with a sandbar of deep, beautiful white sand, perfect for camping in any weather. This is not simply wishful thinking; a sandbar has been creeping upriver along the bank and had arrived almost contiguous to his property. If, as he anticipated, it continued upriver, a real sandy beach would benefit future visitors to Poche Park.

Naturally I wondered what had provoked the river angel to create his riverside welcome center. Had he been a longtime Mississippi River canoeist and was sympathetic to that travel genre? Had he planned to join the roster of river angels?

No, he had neither canoed nor planned his project; it just happened.

Charlie and his indulgent and supportive wife Shirley live in a trim, modern house a few blocks inland from the levee. The once three-hundred-acre tract known as Bellevue Plantation was purchased in the 1920s by Charlie's father at a sheriff's sale and was subsequently subdivided so that most of his neighbors are relatives. Because the property is along the River Road, the ownership of Bellevue included ownership of the batture across the levee.

Charlie had been a longtime shift worker at a local refinery who, according to Shirley, "kept everything running and always did know how to fix and build things." After retiring in 2004, he indulged himself with the purchase of a couple of golf carts to putter about, but that was boring. He then decided it might be fun to ride them over the levee and around the family batture. But the area was so thoroughly wild he was forced to clear out some shrubbery and chop down some trees to create riding trails.

As he rode, he began picking up the flotsam that the river deposited on his bank.

In 2009, Charlie discovered the website of *Big River* magazine, a publication devoted to the Mississippi River, with features about exploring the river, ads for products related to river travel, stories about river adventures, and editorials about improving the river. He was hooked. When he then read a story about paddlers who would soon pass his batture, he impetuously decided to meet them. He contacted the travelers through their website, then drove up to Baton Rouge where they were overnighting, promising to feed them if they would stop in Paulina. "We're Cajuns . . . we welcome people," he offered me by way of explanation.

Unfortunately, the river was too high when they arrived and his batture was underwater. But they pulled out on the nearby sandbar and enjoyed the hospitality of an extended family of Poches—a great big pot of jambalaya, "and all the family ladies made sweets."

That initial meeting was the catalyst for Charlie Poche's new avocation, which became a passion. "I started looking at the Mississippi River Paddlers' Facebook page and the *Big River* site," he explained, to learn when small boats might be approaching. If a river traveler had a journey website, Charlie got in touch, followed his progress down the river, and readied the firewood.

He soon developed a routine. Twice a day ("And sometimes in between," Shirley adds, "depending on what's going on"), he rides a golf cart, jazzily emblazoned with flame designs, the half block to the River Road, then over the levee to his batture. He rides along the trails, picks up junk that the river has deposited, and straightens up at Poche Park. If he knows visitors are coming, he makes sure sufficient firewood is available.

Charlie continues to collect the junk-cum-treasures that the river deposits on his beach, always with an eye to recycling them into something useful. The beams he had laid at the campground for sitting had all washed ashore, as had additional beams that he dragged farther inland to mark the landside entrance to Poche Park. A cluster of colorful round buoys and some fat, cheery turquoise rope that washed up had been transformed into decorations.

Through the years, the river has played havoc with the campground. One year, floodwaters remained so high that Poche Park was out of service for months. Eventually, Charlie realized that when high water is predicted, he must move everything possible up to the levee or it would wash away. Evidence of these flood levels are glaring; he pointed almost proudly, to white bands of water lines ringing the willow trunks. One band was at least five feet above the sand.

Annual visitation to Poche Park reaches about fifty people, according to signatures in the log he leaves at the site. He thinks he has met most of them but acknowledges that the campground has become too popular for him to be able to offer his "guests" dinner or provide them all with other personal services.

To date, Charlie's most unusual visitors were three shrimp boats. They had motored upriver from below New Orleans in 2008 when Hurricane Gustav threatened in the Gulf of Mexico. They pulled into the cove on the downriver side of Poche Park, although Charlie never learned how they knew the cove was there. The boats' crews of Vietnamese fishermen never disembarked at Poche Park, staying onboard their boats that were moored tightly together in the sheltered inlet. They motored off after the hurricane passed. The consummate river host seemed slightly disappointed that he hadn't met them.

But I believe it was their loss: They hadn't been able to appreciate all that Poche Park, at Mile 149, had to offer, and they missed the opportunity to meet the Mississippi River's only Cajun river angel.

7
A Low-Tech Masterpiece

I arrived at the Bonnet Carré control structure on a cold Sunday morning in mid-January 2016 to find an eclectic crowd of several hundred already assembled. People had arrived from New Orleans or drifted in from surrounding areas; they'd parked their cars on a small gravel lot atop a green crescent of levee that created a small bay of the Mississippi River where hard waves slashed at the front of the concrete dam.

A designated lookout had been constructed on the flank of the dam behind a tall, black wrought-iron fence. Small children dashed about, their parents in pursuit, and a few gaggles of women swaddled in winter gear jabbered amongst themselves like a coffee klatch. Old-timers could be heard reminiscing about having seen this show before. But everyone kept a watchful eye so as not to miss the moment they had come for: when the first gates of the Bonnet Carré control structure were opened, and the frothing, roiling, muddy waters of the Mississippi River in flood stage crashed through and flowed into the spillway beyond.

The opening of Bonnet Carré is splendid entertainment for those whose preferences lean to the quirky. I had missed the last show in 2011 so, when it became apparent that unusually high water would compel the U.S. Army Corps of Engineers to open the gates now, I vowed to be there despite the odd timing. High water on the Mississippi River has historically appeared in spring, which is why the term "spring flooding" is part of River Road vernacular.

The event resembles a unique form of open air theater; it is free and also educational, thanks to the Corps, which has thoughtfully provided onsite staff to answer questions and explain the mechanics and mission of the ninety-year-old flood control structure. The mechanics are, simply put, opening sluices across a mile-and-a-half-long concrete dam so that water pours through, into a six-mile-long flared and leveed channel. The mission is to keep downstream levees and the city of New Orleans safe during what is euphemistically known as excessive high water on the Mississippi River.

Whether and when to open these gates are decisions that rest with the president of the Mississippi River Commission, on the recommendation of the Corps's New Orleans district engineers. The goal is to keep the volume of river water at a certain gauge in New Orleans flowing below 1.25 million cubic feet per second or, in lay terms, the equivalent of 20,000 bathtubs emptied simultaneously. Each second. It is encouraging to know that, with all gates open, Bonnet Carré could divert 20 percent of the water from the river, preventing it from reaching New Orleans and other communities downriver.

Controlling the Mississippi River has been the purview of all area governments since the colonial period and has remained a challenge. So when Mark Twain offered his sardonic warning about controlling the river in 1883 in *Life on the Mississippi,* few people in power paid attention. "Man cannot tame that lawless stream," Twain wrote. "[We] might as well bully the comets in their courses . . . as try to bully the Mississippi into right and reasonable conduct." Instead, Congress trusted in the ability of engineers to keep local residents safe with a "levees only" flood control policy. However, the Great Flood of 1927 gave lie to that belief, proving that higher and stronger dikes and deeper dredging could not prevent disaster. Constituents besieged Congress, demanding that the Corps "tame the Mississippi River once and for all."

As it happened, another method of river control had been percolating since 1851; this was to mimic the river's original hydrology, recreate its system by adding outflow channels. Before man arrived and insisted on trying to outsmart the river, numerous streams and bayous, termed "distributaries," had funneled the high water of spring flooding away from this part of the river into the back swamps. By the mid-nineteenth century, the confluences with these streams had been dammed or leveed to placate settlers, who had vehemently objected to reopening them. In 1928, however, when the Mississippi River and Tributaries Project was authorized by Congress, it was determined that manmade, and controlled, equivalents to the distributaries should be created. Bonnet Carré would be one of these. (The site's name, pronounced "Bonny Carry," refers to the nearby river bend that resembled the "square bonnet" local women wore into the 1920s.) It is about thirty miles north of the French Quarter as the crow flies.

The question became where to locate the structure.

Some area residents still believe that Bonnet Carré was built in the wrong place. They note that the preferred site was slightly upriver, in an area already known as Crevasse, the French term for "levee break." The river had crashed through there quite dramatically on several occasions. But, possibly due to politics and local power brokers, an alternate site was selected for building the dam, floodway, and levees. Properties were expropriated from thirty-seven landholders, including four large plantations—Delhomme, Hermitage, Roseland, and Myrtle Land.

The civil engineers tasked with designing Bonnet Carré faced a variety of challenges. Among these was determining how to support the foundation of a concrete dam in mud, with no underlying bedrock. The Corps built an onsite hydraulics lab and went about the work of determining the best design for the dam, figuring out the best formula for creating a double-strength concrete, and solving other technical problems. But, the Corps admitted, these and other issues could only be evaluated when the operation of the completed control structure was tested, and worked . . . or didn't.

The dam took two and a half years to construct; the spillway and levees were finished shortly thereafter. The cost of the project, including one railroad bridge and a highway across the span of the spillway, was $13 million.

The design of the concrete dam was cutting-edge engineering for its time. Three hundred and fifty bays each house twenty removable wooden timbers called needles. (If you do the math, that's seven thousand large pine, creosote-treated beams.) The needles, each measuring eleven feet long and a foot thick, rest vertically, side by side, in the bays. When the river is low, you can see them from the spillway side—a packed line of posts resembling a robust wood fence that leaks a little. They are opened by two fire-engine-red cranes that slide along rails on the top of the dam. With the help of several workers, each crane driver hooks an individual needle, lifts it from its setting, and carefully lays it horizontally across the top of the dam. Water surges through the space where the needle has been removed, roiling and fluming like class III rapids. This is how the "show" starts. The process of removing all the timbers takes thirty-six hours, but in an emergency, crane teams can release twenty timbers simultaneously. This would shorten the time to open the structure to a mere three hours but would result in all of the needles floating away in the current. Fortunately, this has never been necessary.

Running parallel to the rear of the dam is a long concrete weir that resembles a line of giant, upturned teeth and serves as a baffle. This is the visible portion of an expanse of articulated concrete that buffers the immense power of the surging water, to prevent it from gouging craters in the ground as it pours through the opened gates.

In 2016, the Corps opened two hundred and ten gates, then closed them with the same precision. While they were open, visitors trekked daily to the scene for, although they missed the premiere, the surging water crashing through the open bays remained a marvel, as did the watery landscape of the spillway where only treetops were visible.

Some visitors came to fish, positioning themselves along the inside slope of the spillway levee to cast hopeful lines for a silver carp, blue catfish, or bass that might have survived its rough passage through the gates. Occasionally, the Corps had to warn off thrill seekers with kayaks. The drama of rushing water was fascinating enough that even drivers crossing the spillway along Interstate 10 and Airline Highway often slowed down to watch the breadth of muddy water racing to Lake Pontchartrain. In part, it was due to the uniqueness of the event—only the eleventh time the complex had been activated since its completion in 1931. Partial openings had occurred in 1937 and again in 1975, 1997, 2008, and 2011; all gates were opened in 1945, 1950, 1973, 1979, and 1983.

I was charmed, and somewhat amused, when I learned that not much has changed about the actual operation of the project since its 1937 debut. Although the Corps itself relies on the most up-to-date technology in all else, the physical action of opening the bays has remained the same. Nothing is digitized or even much mechanized, which may be why this 1930s engineering marvel was considered worthy of inclusion in the National Register of Historic Places.

Before the dance of the red cranes and the wooden needles can take place, the Corps must officially close the seven-thousand-acre spillway, which is usually a popular public recreation area. Approximately 400,000 annual visitors come to this wild patchwork of habitats—bottomland hardwood forests, grasslands, and cypress swamps where deer, rabbits, alligators, feral pigs, otters, raccoons, and possums have been spotted, as well as a variety of birds. Binocular-toting bird-watchers come to spy hawks, a pair of nesting eagles, night herons, and songbirds. Fishermen and hunters, crawfishers, whooping ATV riders, and dog owners handling their charges in competitive retriever field trials—all share the land with mountain bikers, hobbyists with model airplanes and drones, and naturalists. And every one of them must have been certifiably vacated from the tract well before the river is diverted, converting this flat, wild playground into a broad, deep waterway with a powerful and dangerous current.

One set of folks are never removed from the spillway, however; these are the occupants of two African American cemeteries that were located on the land when it was expropriated. Slaves and their descendants from plantations owned by the Kugler and Kenner families were buried here from the mid-nineteenth century until 1929. After the silt-heavy river water inundated the new spillway in 1937, mud covered the cemeteries, the sediment layering higher with each subsequent opening. This is a serious amount of mud: according to the Corps, approximately nine million cubic yards of sediment are deposited across the length of the spillway each time the bays are opened. (After the waters drain, much of this deposited soil is sold, to be used as fill for commercial land development.)

The sediment had obliterated the existence of the cemeteries until, one day in 1975, workers digging a drainage ditch in the spillway unearthed parts of a coffin and headstone with some human remains. The disinterred objects were ultimately identified as having come from the burial site of a former slave named Sanders Ray, who had been a member of Company H, 10th U.S. Colored Heavy Artillery, in the Union army during the Civil War. The discovery of Mr. Ray's gravesite plus subsequent finds including chunks of iron crosses and metal fencing reminded everyone of the presence of the cemeteries.

The descendants of those buried there met with representatives of the Corps to demand consideration for their loved ones. An archaeological excavation ensued to identify site boundaries of the cemeteries; not surprisingly, additional burial artifacts were unearthed. Ultimately, however, the two cemeteries were marked on Corps of Engineers' maps, and the families agreed that the graves would not need to be relocated. The cemeteries, like the Bonnet Carré dam, were added to the National Register. Today, roads to these sites are barely visible and the sites have never been formally identified or improved, for such additions would simply be washed away when the dam was next opened.

Environmentalists, too, have taken heed of the Bonnet Carré openings, concerned about the effect of introducing muddy freshwater from the Mississippi River into brackish Lake Pontchartrain. They feared harm to both water quality and the diverse animal populations in the lake because, while sediment that drops into the spillway is welcome for replenishing its freshwater habitats, it can be problematic for the lake. The speed of the water's flow and the quantity of dirt introduced to lake water change both its clarity and salinity for up to six months.

The Mississippi River also carries high levels of introduced nutrients from upriver agriculture, which can cause algae blooms in Lake Pontchartrain. This condition—a depletion of oxygen—can result in fish kills. During algae blooms, scientists have observed the migration of populations of speckled trout, redfish, crabs, and shrimp out of the lake. But after the 2016 Bonnet Carré opening, they reported, the fish simply avoided the muddy plume of water by gravitating to Pontchartrain's far shore.

As dramatic and compelling as an opening of the Bonnet Carré structure has become to its public, the event has fortunately remained uncommon. The control structure with its history and technical achievement are impressive enough, however, that the Corps has made its story available even in those ordinary times when the river is behaving. In the Corps of Engineers' small office at the head of the control structure, curious visitors can study exhibits about Bonnet Carré and watch an instructive video depicting how the structure functions and what the site looks like when all bays are opened and the tumultuous water rages between the spillway levees.

This is an entertaining and educational display, I can attest, and certainly an acceptable substitute for the real show that will happen—we hope and pray—oh so rarely.

III

Elegance—Now and Then

8
Buried Treasure

It did not look like a field of dreams when Pinnacle Entertainment bought the old Chatsworth Plantation property. The overgrown tract was dense with Johnsongrass, blackberry brambles, and wildflowers scattered among tall trees and impenetrable shrubbery. A healthy population of cottonmouth snakes added to the flat land's inhospitable character. Perhaps the expanse had once been planted in sugarcane, but that was decades ago. And the grand old Chatsworth house, a fifty-room antebellum mansion, had been demolished so many years before that no one could remember it.

In 2006, Pinnacle surely envisioned success with its L'Auberge Casino Resort in this undeveloped area of suburban Baton Rouge, bringing gaming rooms, restaurants, entertainment venues, and a hotel. But I suspect that no one at Pinnacle ever imagined another, totally unrelated jackpot—namely, discovery of a historic treasure lying undisturbed in those wild fields.

The hidden treasure might have stayed there forever but for an obligation upon the new owners according to Section 106 of the National Historic Preservation Act. This mandates a "cultural resources investigation" before a historic property can be redeveloped. In this case, Pinnacle had to find out if anything of historic value was hidden in those fields before creating a golf course, building a residential neighborhood, or whatever other best use they determined.

Archaeologists knew before excavating that they would find no relics from the Chatsworth house; its location was under the current levee and river bank. But remarkably, the routine investigation that followed became the largest plantation archaeological excavation in Louisiana, according to principal archaeologist Dennis Jones. The fields of Chatsworth turned out to be "an archaeological goldmine, like a time capsule," he enthused. Undisturbed for years, the overgrown acreage revealed surprising evidence of many residents who had occupied Chatsworth for more than a century and a half.

The tract known as Chatsworth had first appeared on early colonial maps as the site of an Alibama Indian village. Naturalist William Bartram visited there in 1775 and described the settlement in his *Travels.* This was affirmed when the dig unexpectedly uncovered Alibaman ceramics made with crushed rangia shells, stone-cutting tools, scrapers, and other Native American objects.

After two decades the Alibama moved on, and the tract was distributed as small Spanish land grants. In 1830, Frenchman Fergus Duplantier consolidated many of these into a single, expansive property—a sugar plantation with a sugar mill added in 1844. Duplantier's nephew and stepson, Fergus Peniston, bought the land from his widowed aunt/stepmother, then added contiguous tracts until he had amassed an even more magnificent estate of eighteen hundred acres which, of course, demanded a lavish mansion.

Peniston named the property Chatsworth, for the eponymous sixteenth-century manor house in Derbyshire, England. His Chatsworth on the Mississippi was similarly impressive. "Palatial in size and magnificent in finish," a nineteenth-century visitor described the classical revival house. Its front façade featured six Corinthian columns and was flanked by symmetrical, galleried wings. Galleries encircled the house. The interior was splendid with ornately carved moldings and plasterwork, a marble staircase and marble mantels, and heavy silver-plated hardware—escutcheoned doorknobs and door hinges among these lavish appurtenances.

Peniston's success as a planter was reflected in the 1860 census, which reported that Chatsworth's assets included 151 slaves who lived in forty-one quarters cabins. The ruins of approximately half of these buildings were revealed in the archaeological dig; they were primarily double-pen—divided by a central hearth with a fireplace open to each side, which served two families under one roof. The brick bases and fireplace bricks from the structures were among the buried treasure revealed. "You can tell the bricks were made here," said Dennis, showing me their rounded edges.

Fergus Peniston lost his fortune in the Civil War and sold Chatsworth in 1865 to a successful French émigré, François Gardere. He set up his son Fergus as property manager. (There seems to have been no relationship between Fergus G. and Fergus P.; it was seemingly mere coincidence that they shared the unusual given name.)

The younger Gardere moved his family into the grand mansion, improved the sugar mill, and instituted tenant farming and sharecropping, to ensure that Chatsworth could continue to grow and mill sugarcane in the new, post–Civil War economy. Fergus G. also quite astutely permitted the Mississippi Valley Railroad to lay track across his acreage, giving his plantation direct access to the rail line between New Orleans and Baton Rouge. Later, he received a spur line from the main track direct to the Chatsworth sugar mill, an additional advantage for delivering his sugar to market.

In 1894, the Garderes sold a half-interest in Chatsworth to Thomas Womack, who purchased the remainder the following year. It was Womack and family who occupied the house in

1898 when the sugar mill burned down. Womack rebuilt a larger mill with a slightly different configuration, and equipped it with the most modern machinery. The sturdy brick base of this mill, with its maze of brick framing for water tanks, furnaces, and other equipment, was the most prominent discovery in Pinnacle's "cultural resources investigation."

Womack sold Chatsworth in 1901 to five investors who incorporated themselves as Chatsworth Planting and Manufacturing. They appointed one member, Leufroy Landry, to serve as property manager, so Landry and his family are most likely the group posed, portrait-style, on Chatsworth's front steps in Andrew Lytle's photograph of Chatsworth that dates from about 1910. Although the family looks rather successful, the mansion, once magnificent, had begun to look dilapidated.

After 1917, ownership of Chatsworth changed several more times, even as sugar was continually farmed in its fields and its mill processed cane. The house continued to deteriorate, and in 1928 a renter was discovered living in a small corner of the cavernous home. He apparently generated income by using the atmospheric old pile as an entertainment venue, especially for hosting parties enjoyed by local university students. According to a 1930 newspaper article, sheriff's deputies raided the house and discovered "more than three hundred bottles of beer, a half pint of gin and a number of crocks," probably for making home brew. This was, of course, during the years of Prohibition.

Although the Great Flood of 1927 did not inundate Chatsworth, the new levee built by the Army Corps of Engineers after the flood was planned exactly where the old house was located; it was unceremoniously demolished. Soon after, the sugar mill fell into disuse, and eventually collapsed on itself. In a 1931 aerial photograph of Chatsworth, the ruins of the mill, as well as a handful of the slave-turned-tenant cabins and two plantation outbuildings, are visible. Sharecroppers apparently still occupied several cabins. Another aerial photo of Chatsworth taken in the early 1950s shows only two cabins, the outbuildings, and mill ruins. By 1986, in the most recent aerial photograph I could find, the property was completely overgrown. No structures were visible. "There was nothing," Dennis Jones observed, "to indicate that Chatsworth Plantation had ever existed."

Until, of course, Pinnacle Entertainment was required to underwrite the archaeological investigation.

The exploration of Chatsworth's fields began in 2006, conducted by the southeastern Louisiana district archaeologist. This was followed by a more formal and targeted investigation from 2010 until 2013, undertaken by Coastal Environments Inc. "It was a jungle," one of that firm's archaeologists said to a reporter. "You wouldn't have known anything was there." Nevertheless, they discovered the sugar mill remains—a sloppy brick wall fenced in by brambles and a stand of young trees—but focused their dig primarily on the site of the old quarters as that was the area Pinnacle had targeted for building a new public roadway.

Dennis Jones was brought into the project after Pinnacle decided to donate the findings from the Chatsworth excavation to the LSU Rural Life Museum. The Baton Rouge museum collects and exhibits artifacts representing Louisiana's working classes and their cultures in "life beyond the big house." The objects from Chatsworth, dating from the eighteenth-century Alibama natives to the mid-twentieth-century tenant farmers, fit right in, offering a timeline of life on the property.

"I lived Chatsworth for five straight years," Dennis Jones confessed. The project represented the culmination of his career in Louisiana archaeology, which had begun in 1986 and included both prehistoric and historic sites for the state's Division of Archaeology as well as his own private firm. The site for LSU was his last gig before official retirement, he had decided; he would turn in his Chatsworth report to Pinnacle and the Louisiana Division of Archaeology at the end of 2017.

To Dennis, archaeology offers the ideal way to interpret history and previous cultures by removing from the ground evidence of those who lived in a place and analyzing how they lived there. Articles that inhabitants broke, lost, or threw away become clues to their lives. Of course, he cautioned me, "you have to be OCD about how you dig . . . about where [in the ground] the artifacts come from [and] the distribution of where they're found." This is the science of the profession, allowing even the smallest particle to contribute to the bigger story. Careful record keeping is imperative, but learning the historical context of the found materials is equally important.

On a scorching summer day, I visited the Chatsworth dig site, following a weedy, single-track dirt road off the public highway. I found Dennis in his trademark Indiana Jones hat, cheeks red with heat and his bright eyes darting about. He was supervising a crew of archaeology students, part of his full team of fourteen which included both students and professionals. As I stepped from the car, one of the infamous snakes slid into the knee-high grass, startling me but not the archaeologists, who had grown to disregard them as distractions. They continued to trowel carefully in meticulously cut rectangular trenches, then brought their haul to sifter screens to separate even the smallest shards from the dirt. This excavation focused on the sites of the former quarters cabins and, when I peered into a trench, I could discern some familiar items in the dirt—a piece of ceramic, a rusty nail. Dennis and his team would interpret these clues in piecing together the puzzle of Chatsworth.

Behind the cabin sites was a large, open area around an arrangement of brick walls—the now-exposed remains of the 1898 sugar mill. The mill had been built upon a concrete floor, and the bricks that remained in place showed its stalwart construction, the thick walls as handsome as those of a plantation house. The mill site had been so overgrown that the archaeologists were forced to use a backhoe to begin uncovering it, he told me. I found this surprising because, in my lay understanding, archaeology consisted of squatting in a trench with a trowel. But the use of heavy machinery is acceptable—even necessary, Dennis explained, especially when the target of a dig is buried beneath "unrelated, non-cultural material." In Chatsworth's case, this meant years of overgrowth and new stands of trees.

By the time the Chatsworth investigation ended, a staggering 173,000 artifacts had been collected. "Most [of the artifacts] are teeny little things," Dennis explained, but much was recognizable: plates, cups, pieces of sugar mill machinery, gear teeth, stirrups, plows, hoe blades, bolts, animal bones—from cows, pigs, chickens, deer. Turtle shells. Metal artifacts such as a 1920s ice cream freezer. And, of course, the unanticipated relics from the Alibama village.

This trove was stored in Dennis's lair, a climate-controlled room tucked off the main exhibit space at the Rural Life Museum. It served as his office throughout the dig—desk and computer, work space, an oversized, specially crafted table for examining artifacts. The room came to resemble a small warehouse, ringed with stacks of shelving nearly to the ceiling, each shelf crammed with banker's boxes inscribed according to their contents. A contiguous room served as a lab where electrolysis was performed on metal objects to remove rust. All this was part of Pinnacle's investment in the Chatsworth project—more than a million dollars, which underwrote the salaries of the professional archaeologists, the excavations, the facilities, and the digitization and archiving of all relevant documents. Plus production of a YouTube video, to make the findings available to a twenty-first-century public.

Some Chatsworth treasures remain on view at the museum. Several photo montages explain the procedure of the dig, and a few vitrines exhibit Chatsworth's most recognizable artifacts: whole glass bottles from the early twentieth century, a leg from a mid-nineteenth-century china doll, pitcher fragments dating to the late eighteenth or early nineteenth century, a large portion of a handsome platter dating from the first half of the nineteenth century; bone buttons, iron tools, stoneware jugs, a late-nineteenth-century beer bottle, and a few early 1930s soft drink bottles.

Pinnacle seemed pleased with the result of the mandatory investigation. "We were glad that the remaining history of Chatsworth could be brought to life and shared with the community," marketing director Kim Ginn told me, pleased about the partnership with the museum. During the dig, she admitted, some of Pinnacle's administrators had wandered over, just to see the activity taking place within their wild acreage. After the excavation ended, their formal commemoration of Chatsworth was a designated meeting room called the Chatsworth Room, where a photograph of the old plantation house hangs prominently on one wall. I asked Kim what would become of the land now; their property consists of five hundred acres, and the existing gaming and entertainment complex uses only eighty of them. She said they hadn't decided.

I rode past the dig site almost two years after the archaeologists left and saw that the land was still open and undeveloped, although it had been mowed and transformed into a controlled green space. Decorative trees had been planted near the road and the old dirt track to the quarters area and the mill had become a faint trace, almost completely greened over.

But toward the rear of the tract, I spied a mound of dense shrubbery, asymmetrical and lumpy, meaningless to most passersby along the road. I recognized it: the ruins of the sugar mill, again overgrown and hidden. The last visible evidence that Chatsworth Plantation had ever existed was gone once more.

9

Encore for Ashland

I remember my first tour of Ashland/Belle Helene. It was a wintry day in the late 1980s, and I had spied a small sign at the intersection of the River Road and LA 3251 inviting visitors to tour the elegant, columned box of a mansion visible from the road. Belle Helene—beautiful Helene, set in a green landscape surrounded by huge live oaks. So I drove into the property, barely noticing the unkempt grounds, and parked in the designated grassy area at the rear of a large house that had once been the jewel of an extensive sugar plantation.

A disheveled, khaki-clad man, an older gent as I recall, requested an admission fee, then led me across the expansive back gallery. Before we entered the house, I noticed the massive pillars and looming façade were mottled with mildew and grime. The interior was dim and sparsely furnished with vintage furniture and some decorative objects, all dwarfed by the grandeur of the rooms. We skirted several of the downstairs chambers because the floors had been removed, revealing dirt. I asked if an archaeological dig was underway. It was not, he tersely replied, without elaboration.

As we meandered through the once-splendid house, my

guide proudly pointed out unique architectural features—intricate moldings, the elegantly carved banister that traced a graceful oval staircase—and tossed out tidbits of plantation history. But I admit I was too focused on the discolored plaster on the walls, grinning gaps in the crown molding, and the overall derelict condition of the house to absorb much of what he said. Only many years later did I learn that my docent that day was a member of the family who had owned the house since 1889.

It was apparent from my tour that this onetime grande dame of the River Road had devolved into a classical revival bag lady and I supposed she would ultimately suffer the fate of so many River Road mansions: it would deteriorate to the point that it must be demolished, leaving only photographs for future generations.

This fear, I am happy to report, was misplaced.

Today, the old mansion stands elegantly, almost radiantly, reigning over her green, tree-shaded corner. She is again called Ashland (sometimes Ashland/Belle Helene) and has been restored, both inside and out, to look much like her glory days when the dashing young planter and businessman Duncan Kenner built the magnificent home in 1841. But perhaps the most surprising aspect of this story is the identity of Ashland's unlikely savior: the Shell Chemical Company.

The chemical giant had eyed the Belle Helene tract since it opened its Geismar plant in 1967 on adjoining property. When the company finally negotiated the purchase in 1992, it acquired 102 acres including the deteriorating house. And, as Shell would have been the first to admit, its interest in the property had little to do with historic preservation. But one condition of the purchase agreement was the requirement to maintain the historic building's exterior and never to demolish it. For the first time in decades, the old house would be stabilized and secured, though it would remain closed and empty for almost twenty years.

And then Shell decided to restore the interior, to utilize Ashland/Belle Helene as a venue for company meetings and conferences. The renovation of the house became a source of pride for both the Shell Chemical Company and the River Road community. The sequence was almost like a modern fairy tale.

Sugar planter and businessman Duncan Farrar Kenner, scion of a grand New Orleans family, spared no expense in building the mansion for his bride, Anne Guillemine "Nanine" Bringier. He named the house "Ashland" in honor of Henry Clay's Kentucky plantation; he was a great admirer of the Whig Party founder. Kenner hired either James Dakin or James Gallier Sr. as architect, although definitive proof of which renowned designer deserves the credit has never been verified. Regardless, the result was an imposing and elegant house that ranks as one of the purest expressions of Greek revival architecture in Louisiana, according to architectural historians. Its boxy appearance, unusual to the River Road, derives from the parapet—the short wall crowning the roofline—that rises above the single row of columns surrounding the house on all four sides, in the peripteral style. The parapet hides the roof peak, creating the appearance of the house as a lovely symmetrical box.

Ashland's exterior walls, painted a soft butter yellow, were crafted sixteen inches thick, brick overplastered with a stucco-cement scored to resemble sandstone. Each of its twenty-eight Doric columns was constructed of plastered brick, three feet square, and painted white. The columns rise thirty feet high, the full two stories.

Soaring fourteen-foot ceilings define ground-floor spaces; twelve-and-a-half-foot ceilings grace the bedroom floor. Downstairs in the original home were a double parlor, dining room, office, and library. The latter measured more than twenty feet square and was reported by a contemporary to be "one of the most beautiful rooms south of the Mason-Dixon line." A twelve-foot-wide center hallway runs front to back on each floor;

fireplaces in each room were set off by mantels of imported Italian marble, even those upstairs in the four gracious bedrooms.

Like other antebellum River Road plantations, Duncan Kenner's Ashland was a small community, from the river landing and warehouse at the levee to the big house to numerous outbuildings—kitchen, pigeonniers and garçonnières, a plantation office, a double row of thirty-five slave cabins, a school, an infirmary, and dozens of other utility buildings such as storehouses and barns. A massive sugar mill loomed over all. At the height of his career, Kenner owned several sugarcane plantations totaling 2,200 acres; his mills produced over two million pounds of sugar. The labor was provided by almost five hundred slaves.

Kenner was also an avid horseman and breeder. Before the Civil War, he owned as many as fifty thoroughbreds and celebrated some of his best with oil portraits hung on Ashland's walls, many of which were painted by the prominent equine artist Edward Troye. Kenner had developed a mile-long oval racetrack on the property, which provided the source for an amusing if apocryphal story: One evening, guests had left Ashland after a late dinner and their coachman, who was unfamiliar with the Kenner plantation, got confused in the dark. He drove in circles around and around the racetrack for quite some time before discovering his error. Remains of Kenner's famous and well-used oval were said to be visible near the cane fields for nearly a century.

Duncan Kenner had begun his professional life reading law and learning about politics in the office of John Slidell, so it was not surprising that he pursued public life in tandem with his career as a planter. He was a member of the Louisiana legislature and, after secession, became a well-respected member of the Confederate Congress, sent by Jefferson Davis as special minister to England and France to seek support for the Confederacy. (He was unsuccessful.)

During the war, Union soldiers seized Ashland and stole the prized horses as well as cattle, supplies, hogsheads of sugar, the family silver, and much more. A terrified Nanine fled with the children to Natchitoches. But fortunately, and perhaps surprisingly, the soldiers did not burn Kenner's grand mansion, turning it over instead to the Freedmen's Bureau, from which Kenner reclaimed it in 1866.

After the war, the Kenners' primary residence was in New Orleans, but the master of Ashland rebuilt his River Road properties. He was a respected leader in the sugar industry and helped organize the Louisiana Sugar Planters Association. By the 1880s, Kenner's assets were reputedly greater than they had been before the Civil War, but this was apparently due in large measure to clever real estate investments rather than to the sugar business. When he died in 1887, he was widely mourned.

Nanine sold Ashland two years later to George B. Reuss, also a sugar planter with multiple properties. Reuss renamed the property Belle Helene in honor of his granddaughter. He had bought it for its extensive fields, never intending to live there as he was comfortable at his family plantation, Germania, located across the river. Although members of the Reuss family occasionally lived in the mansion, their energies were primarily focused on sugar and rice production.

In 1911, Reuss decided to subdivide and sell much of Belle Helene's acreage. Thereafter, the house was seldom occupied; by the 1920s, a visiting journalist described it as abandoned and falling into disrepair.

After the eponymous Helene married William Hayward, members of the family attempted various restoration projects on the house. One architectural historian who visited deemed the efforts "badly executed," and Harnett Kane, in his 1945 book, *Plantation Parade,* described the house as sitting "empty and forgotten . . . weather-stained, untended, the parade of the tall pillars has taken on a dingy tone, and the floors of the great galleries are collapsing at the corners." Sadly, I could have written a similar description after my tour in the late 1980s.

The empty house was wracked by the occasional hurricane

and attracted vandals. The most egregious incident occurred in 1959 when a group of area teenagers broke in and went "wilding," destroying all the original marble mantels, adding to the insults that neglect had already brought. Black-and-white photos taken in the late 1950s show fireplaces stripped of mantels, walls grimy and moldy, woodwork pocked with peeling paint. The floor of a second-story gallery angles downward like a slide; the flooring of another gallery is stripped to the joists. The bases of the giant columns are ringed with crumbled bricks and rubble.

Despite the dereliction, or perhaps because of it, filmmakers had discovered Belle Helene to be an atmospheric set. *Band of Angels,* starring Clark Gable (1957), *The Beguiled,* starring Clint Eastwood (1971), *Mandingo,* starring James Mason (1975), and *Fletch Lives,* starring Chevy Chase (1989) were partially filmed there. Somewhat ironically, the plot of *Fletch Lives* involves an heir to a supposedly fine old plantation who arrives to claim his property and finds it rundown and long neglected. That was Belle Helene, although she had been enrolled in the National Register of Historic Places a decade before.

A family feud exacerbated the problems involved with ownership as William Hayward Jr. and John Hayward and their niece, Joan Hayward McKee, sued Helene and her son Douglas over mismanagement of Germania Plantation Inc. Joan McKee professed to love the Belle Helene house and told interviewers that she tried to help save it, spearheading an effort to replace the roof. For this project, she had raised a $5,000 donation from the new neighbor, Shell Chemical, to match a federal grant. At the time, Shell Chemical's plant manager commented, "We all have an interest in the place." McKee's husband, a son, and his friends did the roofing, sleeping first on the home's broad gallery, then in a small camper hauled onto the property. Soon after, William Hayward Jr. moved his own trailer onto the property, and the quarrel escalated.

Shell Chemical Company negotiated with the Haywards for nineteen years before paying $3 million for the property, a sum that was reported at the time to be five times the appraised value. Joan McKee regretted the sale, lamenting, "If we [the family members] had gotten along and worked together, then Belle Helene would not be gone."

This was a familiar problem along the River Road, according to the Louisiana Office of Historic Preservation. Divided ownership of a property within an extended family often leads to the demise of many a grand mansion and its sale because family members can't agree about what to do or how to take care of it.

The sale of Belle Helene concerned the local preservation community for another reason: they had harbored suspicion and animosity toward the petrochemical industry ever since Marathon Oil Company had, they believed, double-crossed them. Marathon had bought San Francisco Plantation and donated it to a nonprofit foundation, but then bulldozed Welham Plantation while negotiations with preservationists about the fate of that old house were still ongoing. The bitterness from that episode hung over the River Road like a toxic fume.

One term of the sale agreement stipulated that the Haywards could repurchase the house and thirty-four contiguous acres, contingent on their raising $1.5 million through a new nonprofit, to be accomplished within four months of the sale. They couldn't, and Shell Chemical Company became the third owner of one of the finest examples of antebellum homes ever built on the River Road.

The sale appeared to be successful for both sides. The Hayward family received money to settle their debts and buy out disgruntled shareholders; Shell acquired land for its plant expansion, a facility to produce ethylene oxide and ethylene glycol. And Shell would restore Belle Helene's exterior, stabilize the interior, and never tear down the mansion. The National Trust for Historic Preservation optimistically called the sale "a noble gesture."

The new owner repainted the exterior in its original colors: pale butter-yellow walls, gleaming white columns. They re-roofed, upgraded the electrical system, cleansed the interior walls of mold, and treated for termites; security systems were installed and a large tank erected as a ready water supply in case of fire. Shell also bought salvaged flooring from a mid-nineteenth-century New Orleans school to replace the dirt floors in the several downstairs rooms.

A professional horticulturist cleared and pruned the old oaks and exterior lighting was introduced, which not only added security but also enhanced the appearance of the old place. From the road, "it made the house glow like a jewel," a delighted neighbor enthused; *Preservation in Print* magazine agreed. And, Shell's plant manager noted, an unexpected result was that employees suddenly became conversant about antebellum architecture. "The house really grows on you," he admitted.

Shell was required to underwrite an archaeological excavation of the grounds, which focused on the area around the old sugar mill and slave quarters. Twenty-one boxes of artifacts were unearthed and donated to the State Historic Preservation Office—fragments of glass and ceramics, pipe bowls, bones, doll fragments, buttons, game pieces, and more. These and a publication about the findings provided a tangible history of Ashland/Belle Helene from Duncan Kenner until after World War I.

And that fulfilled Shell's obligations. The house would not be open to the public like other River Road plantation houses, although the new owners allowed visits by academics, historians, and a few preservation groups, and held the occasional event for employees at the site. Although the company publicly stated that Ashland/Belle Helene was "an asset and an important part of the heritage of local community and state," it was, in truth, their antebellum albatross.

This began to change in 2013 when a new "maintenance and turnaround manager," as Bobby Otterstetter's position was titled, inherited oversight of the elegant, empty plantation house among his responsibilities. As it happened, Bobby loved old buildings and vintage furnishings. "The first time I went in the house, it broke my heart," he remembered. Though the house had been stabilized, the walls and flooring "looked industrial." Not long after, he attended an event at nearby Houmas House, another imposing historic home that had recently been painstakingly restored, furnished, and opened to the public. Impressed, Otterstetter asked the owner of Houmas House to come to Ashland and offer suggestions about how Shell might fix up its interior.

A small team of knowledgeable folks with experience in historic architecture and restoration arrived at Ashland and gave Shell Chemical a laundry list of what could be done, including estimates of cost. The roster of improvements included repairing original woodwork—doors, moldings, and baseboards—repairing and refinishing the floors, replacing fireplace mantels, removing added walls and doors, and much more. It would be a considerable undertaking.

The maintenance and turnaround manager approached Shell's general manager with the list, its cost, and a practical suggestion: since the plant didn't have adequate space to accommodate larger meetings and sometimes had to rent trailers, why not restore Ashland and use it instead?

The plant manager agreed and also queried employees, who were enthusiastic. Shell decided to restore the house to something like its mid-nineteenth-century grandeur, capturing the soul of Duncan Kenner's mansion but for use as a practical, twenty-first-century venue.

The project began in late 2014 under the supervision of a preservation architect and executed by experienced craftsmen. "I bet there's not a square inch inside that wasn't touched," Bobby told me proudly. He pointed to a digitized display on a sideboard in the downstairs hall that scrolls through photographs showing Ashland's appearance before Shell began its work—the house almost exactly as I had seen it.

The restoration was extensive. The long-damaged plaster walls were repaired, the crown moldings were repaired or reproduced. Greek revival window moldings were restored, and mantels of marble similar to the originals were created for the fireplaces. Antique and reproduction chandeliers recalling the original owner's taste were hung from restored medallions on the high ceilings.

"Time-appropriate" furnishings were selected to accommodate Shell's gatherings. One day when I visited, an expansive, antique dining room table, almost spanning the length of Duncan Kenner's grand double parlor, was covered with open laptops and coffee cups and ringed with men and women engaged in intent conversation. Bathrooms, a prep space and a small warming kitchen, digital connectivity, and more sophisticated security systems were also added. A new entrance and driveway lead to a defined parking lot at the rear of the house, protecting the magnificent live oaks that once shaded Kenner and his family.

Upstairs bedrooms were furnished with vintage tester beds and appropriate pieces, some of which date to the era of Reuss/Hayward ownership. "The family had offered to sell [the furniture] in 1992," Bobby had learned, but Shell had balked at the asking price. Eventually, the family reduced the price. "And we think two [of our pieces of furniture] may even be from Duncan Kenner," he said hopefully.

The contrast with the house I saw in the late 1980s is breathtaking. The brick herringbone floors of the first floor galleries and the soft butter-yellow, scored-stucco exterior are immaculately finished; the grand square columns encircling the house and the parapet are pristine. On the interior, original baseboards almost a foot high, the wide door frames, and elaborate crown moldings are spotless; the chandeliers sparkle. The mellow old-pine floorboards are polished, and the plastered walls are painted in period colors. Even the oval staircase has been restored as a jewel of fine craftsmanship. When I wandered onto the upstairs back gallery, I looked out into the thick canopy of oaks, and back in time.

According to Kevin Hardy, Shell Chemical's community relations manager, the investment has paid off well. The house is a much-used meeting space and the site for company functions such as retirement parties. But, ever conscious of public expectations, Shell had continued to ponder a way to create some kind of regular visitor access, while adhering to the absolute caveat that Ashland would never be open for routine tours.

Not long after Shell began restoring the interior of Ashland, I heard rumors that preservation purists objected that this iconic River Road mansion would not be returned to perfect antebellum splendor and opened as a member of the plantation parade. But I personally am grateful that Ashland/Belle Helene will never again suffer from the vandalism, neglect, and ravages of time that could lead to its demolition and that she is again a grande dame of the River Road.

According to a clear-eyed analysis of such situations by a National Trust spokesman in 1992, "some kind of public-private partnership is probably the only realistic way to save some of these properties." For Ashland/Belle Helene, her highly unlikely white knight was the Shell Chemical Company.

10

Replanting a Plantation House

Here is a classic River Road story with all the requisite ingredients: family, property, and history, seasoned with a dash of River Road lore.

It is not unusual along the River Road to move a building. Structures of many kinds have been set back or relocated since early settlement. Neither is it uncommon to adapt a historic building into a livable, twenty-first-century space; after all, there is an unmistakable charm in living or working in a vintage building. Nor is it unknown for such a project to become an obsession.

Norman Marmillion has just the sort of quixotic streak to have undertaken such a project. In his case, the building was a late-eighteenth-century Creole house that had belonged to his (very) extended family since its construction. And although he and his wife Sand had already put heart and soul into creating the complex that is Laura Plantation, it was not in Norman's family. The new venture, however, was entirely personal: he and Sand would move and restore the old Columbia plantation house, which, when completed, would be their River Road residence.

Sand, the more clear-eyed of the twosome, knew that even after their approximately six-year investment of time, money, and labor, and even after they had moved in, Columbia would probably never be truly finished. "Historic preservation," she murmured, "is extremely masochistic."

When the Marmillions purchased Columbia, it was a one-story cottage, painted a soft yellow and seeming to be in the classical revival style. The house was located on its original property, just upriver from St. John Catholic Church in Edgard; it boasted a grand allée of towering old live oaks that marched from its rear yard downriver to the church.

Originally, the house was constructed for Magdelaine Haydel Becnel and her husband, Pierre Becnel, around 1785. It was a small, raised Creole cottage, two rooms across, measuring a mere thirty by forty feet, according to Norman. As prosperity came to its owners, the home was greatly enlarged, and in the only surviving photograph of this grander house, a Robert Tebbs image from 1922, it has become predictably Creole. It is handsome though not imposing, with a ground floor façade finished with plaster (apparently discolored) where storage, offices, and the like would have been housed. The second story, always the living area in Creole houses, appeared to be wood frame, at least on the side revealed to Tebbs's camera. Columns and galleries decorated the front and rear of the house that was covered by a high, hipped roof defined by two chimneys. Several dependencies, in varying states of disrepair, occupied the grounds. At the time of the photograph, Columbia was clearly a bit shopworn.

The most significant moment in family history, according to Norman, occurred in 1801, when the widowed Magdelaine traded her property—then called Becnel Place—with her sister Françoise Haydel. Françoise had married Pierre E. B. Marmillion; these were Norman's "great-great-great-grandparents," making Magdelaine his great-great-great-aunt. (There may even be a "great" missing . . .) The Becnels and Marmillions were close and interrelated families who cooperated in agricultural pursuits as well as daily life, to the extent that their respective livestock were permitted to roam freely between their properties and that of a third close neighbor.

In 1828, Valsin P. B. Marmillion, son of Françoise and Pierre, bought out his two brothers to amass eleven arpents' frontage (along the river), defining his prosperous sugar plantation then known as the Marmillion place. J. W. Dorr, traveling through St. John the Baptist Parish in 1860, did not mention the Marmillion place when he spotlighted impressive homes in the area. However, "V. B. Marmillion" was included among Dorr's roster of the "heavy planters" of the parish.

In 1870 L. D. Martin purchased the Marmillion place, renaming it "Matilda." His descendants who lived there until 1891 seemed to prefer its previous designation, however; when Martin's stepson, J. B. Graugnard, and his partner E. T. Caire bought the property in 1892, it was referred to as the Marmillion place. Then, after an 1893 visit to the World's Fair in Chicago, Graugnard and Caire changed the plantation's name to Columbia because the fair, officially known as the Chicago World's Fair and Columbian Exposition, celebrated the four-hundredth anniversary of Christopher Columbus's arrival in the New World. Columbia Plantation, both house and land, remained in the Graugnard family until distant cousin Norman Marmillion purchased the house.

The fields of what became Columbia Plantation had grown sugarcane since the early days; its mill, last known as Caire & Graugnard, produced both raw sugar and "plantation refined sugar." The latter was somewhat unusual—a product of white crystals coarser than refined sugar, used in candies, confections, and syrup. The Columbia mill continued to operate until 1996.

After the Great Flood of 1927, the appearance of the house changed dramatically. Rebuilding the levee after the flood required that the house be rolled back on its tract, so its owners moved the second story. They reduced the old Creole house to one story, raised on short piers. The Corps had assured the family that they didn't need to raise the house to two floors again; the new levee would protect them. So Columbia became a single story which, as seen in a drawing by the Historic American Buildings Survey, had a spacious, railed front gallery with a bank of French doors and a single chimney emerging from the center of the roof, which was in the Creole style. These alterations were dramatic enough that in the 1941 WPA *Guide to Louisiana,* directing tourists to local attractions, Whitney and Evergreen plantation houses and the Caire Store were mentioned, but Columbia was not included.

In 1983, Norman and Sand attended a reunion of the very extended Marmillion/Haydel family. A mind-boggling seven hundred members of the clan gathered in Edgard and New Orleans to celebrate the two-hundredth anniversary of Françoise and Pierre's wedding. Norman approached his distant cousin, the current owner of Columbia, and offered to buy the house. He envisioned restoring the family home, rebuilding a ground floor comparable to the original, then surrounding the restored Creole house with special gardens of plantings that reflected early ethnic cultures of the area. The house, however, was currently rented.

Then, in 2011, the call came: Norman could buy the house and a small tract around it. But the offer did not include enough property for the gardens he envisioned, so he decided he would buy the old Becnel/Marmillion/Matilda/Columbia house and move it to another piece of property. Which, at the time, he didn't own.

Almost serendipitously, he soon received an offer for open land on the downriver boundary of Whitney Plantation from its owner, John Cummings. This presented Norman a River Road site that was not too far from Laura; he had only to make plans to physically transport the house the four short miles up the River Road.

Moving a historic house is always a challenge, I have been told. In fact, the website of one house-moving company prompts prospective customers to consider whether moving the house makes financial and logistical sense. Would it be cheaper, the website asks, to move the house or to build a new one? But this was never a factor in Norman's decision. So it should not have been surprising, as the logistics of the move were researched, when he learned that Columbia, even with roof removed, would be too large to pass through particular spots along the route, where fences and trees crowded too close to the two-lane highway.

The short four miles stretched to thirteen as the house, strapped atop a truck bed, was forced to head down River Road to LA 640 in Edgard, turned west to LA 3127, then east on LA 3213, then downriver again along the River Road. Five right turns. And, as the family home began its passage, it lumbered past the church cemetery in Edgard where Françoise was buried. "Your house is passing by your tomb," Norman silently told Françoise.

He had hired a truck to precede the rolling house, to pull up signs that were too close to the roads, then replace them; to lean telephone poles away from the traveling cottage and stretch barbed wire fences. The roof, divided into pieces and numbered, was moved separately. In May of 2012, after a tortuous journey, the Columbia plantation house arrived at its new home without a scratch.

Restoration proceeded slowly as Norman and Sand gathered information and sorted out which of the historic elements of the house were serviceable. The Tebbs photograph furnished a blueprint for determining how high the ground floor should be rebuilt under the remaining house. Archival research revealed architectural secrets such as the existence of columned side galleries with a dentil frieze that had been added to the house in the 1850s, then removed after the 1929 setback. Paint scrapings exposed an original façade painted yellow and blue.

Original cypress columns had been stored under the house before it was moved; they were salvaged for the front and rear upstairs galleries. Each column was a turned first-growth cypress trunk capped with a simple Doric capital. Old lumber and unused old brick were also reclaimed from the original site. A visit with an elderly woman who had lived at Columbia half a century before offered Norman clues to how the spaces had been arranged, suggesting a plan for the spaces of his new first floor. In this modern reconstruction, the new ground floor walls are built of cinderblock and finished with plaster; they now enclose an office, a living area, and a mudroom for cleaning up after working in the gardens. There is also access to an elevator as he and Sand plan to grow old here.

The restoration of Columbia brought both delight and challenges. When the existing tin roof was dismantled before the move, Norman discovered an older shingled roof and sites of earlier dormers so he had them reconstructed. The galleries were still adorned with a plastered wall, original wainscoting, door transoms, and full-length shutters; original glass still filled many panes in the old French doors. Four handsome wood mantels original to the house, each one delicately fluted, could be refinished and used. One mantel had previously been donated to Destrehan Plantation, which graciously returned it. And when a modern floor covering was pulled away, the old wood planking was revealed, easy to refinish.

The most unexpected challenge was the need to construct a twenty-eight-inch-thick foundation, a slab more than two feet high. Today, standard concrete slabs for residential construction are usually no thicker than six inches, but Columbia's original walls, now the walls of the Marmillions' second floor, were constructed with the Creole *briquette-entre-poteaux* building technique. Walls of brick stabilized between posts are extremely heavy, and the oversized slab was required to prevent the "new" house from sinking into the ground.

When I walked through the unfinished rooms and saw the exposed walls of soft pink, tightly laid, handmade bricks held fast within diagonal and horizontal hand-hewn beams and notched posts, I was dazzled. I assumed the owners would leave the walls exposed, but Norman corrected me. "This is our home," he replied. "It won't be a museum." Sheetrock would cover the brick. Nevertheless, the entrance to the house would remain as his ancestors designed it, in the rear, according to Creole tradition.

The exterior color scheme of the new house would be eye-popping, although Norman assured me it was reproduced from paint scrapings. Creole buildings have been characterized as having a "fearless use of color," so Columbia's exterior color scheme seems reasonable. Walls of the ground floor are painted French marine blue, with turquoise shutters trimmed in ocher, and white columns. On the second story, the façade is yellow ocher; green shutters and white trim surround the French doors. The original wainscoting on the plastered wall of the second floor gallery and its chair rail are dove gray; the wainscot is inset with rectangles of pale yellow traced by a soft apple green. The railing is two-toned with white balusters and a brick red handrail.

The old/new Columbia plantation house contains approximately seventy-five hundred square feet of living area, including the spacious front and rear galleries. These, according to Norman, must be counted because in a Creole-style building galleries are its only hallways. The "new" house is large, airy, and livable. "This is my family's house," he reflected. It is not only where he and Sand will live, but also "where so many people were born and died. . . . this house has so many stories."

And I feel sure that Norman, the raconteur, will share them all, because the stories bundled inside Françoise's house have moved up the road, too.

IV

Miscellany

11
A Sweet Story

It was the kind of chilly, wet December Sunday that I might have spent curled up inside with a book. But Charlie Schudmak, the fourth-generation owner of the Cora Texas Sugar Factory in White Castle, had agreed that I could tour the mill that day and I very much wanted to see it: Cora Texas is the last working sugar mill along the River Road.

December is the end of crunch time in the sugar business. From the last weeks of October through December, and sometimes even into mid-January, the mill steams and rumbles and hisses all day, every day, through three shifts of workers, until no more sugarcane is brought from the fields. In south Louisiana, this part of the calendar has its own name: grinding season.

This was why, when I arrived, the muddy road into the Cora Texas mill felt a bit like rush hour. My car was dwarfed among the giant eighteen-wheelers with their metal-mesh basket trailers loaded with cut green cane stalks. The trucks splashed through puddles across a wide lot, looking as if they were trying to edge each other out. But as we neared the weigh station, they lined up as dutifully as first-graders, preparing to roll across the scale and then proceed to the core sampler. The latter, a spindly metal frame supporting a mechanical metal tube, is the most critical instrument to cane farmers because it bores into each load, extracting a random sample of cane for lab analysis, which determines the worth of the load.

Beyond the core sampler, each basket trailer dumps its contents onto a conveyor belt and, as the cane streams upward to the crusher, the emptied truck rumbles back across the muddy lot, off to the fields for another load. As many as seven hundred trucks arrive at Cora Texas each day during grinding season, Charlie told me.

But I wouldn't have had to follow the truck traffic to locate Cora Texas. The mill's distinctive industrial architecture was visible at a distance, dominating the flat landscape. And during grinding season, it emits towering clouds of white steam streaming high in the air that obscure the mill's tall, cylindrical stack, painted with fading letters down its height: CORATEXAS.

Sugar mills have been part of the River Road since the early eighteenth century. Eventually, almost every plantation home was the genteel face of an industrial complex that grew and processed cane. Even smaller farmers had mills. The large, noisy sugarhouses transformed the long green stalks of cane into golden-brown crystals of raw sugar and molasses, making the River Road one of the wealthiest areas of the country before the Civil War. After the war, with fields and mills destroyed and the slave labor that had supported the industry freed, many mills never reopened. Of the twelve hundred sugar mills operating in Louisiana before the Civil War, only one hundred and seventy-five survived.

After the Civil War, the remaining sugar factories began to centralize so that one mill served several plantations instead of only its own. By 1949, this trend had reduced the number of working mills along the River Road to fifteen; by 1990, only five remained. And today, although the tall stacks of other sugar mills still rise above the River Road landscape—Cinclare, St. James, McCall—their machinery is silent, leaving Cora Texas the sole River Road operator and one of only eleven sugar mills working in all of Louisiana. Despite this, sugar remains part of what defines the culture of the River Road, just as it has throughout the area's history.

According to the American Sugar Cane League, the association that represents growers, millers, and refiners, the loss of factories simply reflects the increased efficiency of mechanization and sophisticated technology. Charlie Schudmak, knowing the history of the mill that has been the family business since 1919, agreed. "Consolidation is where the growth is," he pronounced. He is CFO of the Cora Texas Manufacturing Company, his first cousin is CEO, and "our fifth generation is just out of diapers," he quipped. His family shares mill ownership with two other families, and they believe that "you either grow or go out of business." The Cora Texas mill has been expanded several times and now processes cane from forty-five thousand acres in several parishes. "Machines haven't replaced workers," Charlie said in defense of this growth. "They've simply made it possible for the same number of operators to handle more volume."

In the old days, cane arrived from the fields on privately owned, narrow-gauge railways. Cora Plantation owned a five-mile track, two locomotives, and seventy-five cars; after its mill burned, the owners added more track to take the cane to a nearby mill. In the 1920s, when state roads were improved, sugar producers discovered that trucks were much more efficient transportation than cane trains; they could drive into the fields to load, saving time and money. By the late 1940s, the little railroads had disappeared, and the eighteen-wheelers with their basket trailers became the emblem of grinding season.

Sugar is such a common foodstuff that I am always astonished to be reminded how complicated it is to produce. And despite the new technologies and digitization of a modern sugarhouse, the operation still follows the same steps and principles used since the earliest days when Etienne de Boré first granulated sugar using four open kettle boilers. Cane stalks are still crushed to extract the juice; the juice is heated, clarified, filtered, evaporated, then crystallized. Success is still called a "strike" and occurs when a sugar maker can affirm that proper-sized granules have been produced.

I was fortunate to see the fascinating inner workings of the sugar mill; most people will never get to do so. "At Cora Texas, we get tourists who drive over from Nottoway, hoping to be able to come through," Charlie noted apologetically. "But it's too dangerous." After my tour, I understood. I had been forced to pay painstaking attention to my guide's instructions as to where to plant each footstep as we climbed slippery metal staircases, trod damp floors, and wound through a complex labyrinth of industrial machinery. Concern for safety in the mill remains the highest priority, a principle reinforced by the hard hat I was mandated to wear, and not as a fashion accessory.

The Cora Texas offices are in a large, unpretentious prefab metal building in the shadow of the roaring mill. The centerpiece of the boardroom is a handsome table fabricated of old wood planks. The antique tabletop is in sharp contrast with the sixty-five-inch video screen that hangs on an end wall of the room that can display, with the click of a remote, color-coded, digitized moving diagrammatics of mill operations, in real time.

Charlie had deputized Adrian Monge to be my guide. Adrian, a chemical engineer from Costa Rica, served for many years as Cora Texas's fabrication superintendent—or, he explained with a grin, "chief engineer in charge of machinery." Following each grinding season, crews must clean, repair, and upgrade equipment to ensure it is ready for the demands of the next grinding season. Now, however, after retiring in 2009, Adrian has achieved the title of fabrication consultant; he returns from Costa Rica only during grinding season.

First stop on the tour: the lab, which is the science brain of the operation, located in a tight space down the hall from the boardroom. This is where the core samples extracted from each truckload of cane are analyzed. A dozen workers, pinned to a variety of small hand-worked and digital machines, determine the quality of sucrose from each sample. The cores, resembling cakes of mud with leaves, are pressed between metal plates at three thousand pounds, to separate the juice from the dry, fibrous plant residue, called bagasse, which resembles garden mulch. The juice is spun to remove the mud from the cut stalks, called billets. After several more steps, the purified juice is run through a polariscope, a small cylinder balanced horizontally in a frame. When shot through with a light beam, the sucrose reading is revealed, typically ranging between 10 and 15 percent. This is the basis for determining the monetary value of each truckload of cane.

When we go from lab to mill, I am dazzled. The sugar factory is a steaming, noisy, two-story warehouse-style building, cavernous, with part of one side open. The interior is filled with an arrangement of imposing equipment in a variety of shapes and sizes—enormous vats, miles of insulated wires, and a mind-numbing collection of tubes and gauges. I followed Adrian to an overlook where the conveyor belts bring the cane stalks up from the trucks. The belts, bearing cane as dense as a mat, drop their load into the jaws of large, whirring, bladed steel drums. These machines chop the stalks, then crush them to squeeze out the juice, which here resembles fluid mud.

In modern sugarhouses like Cora Texas, the fibrous bagasse is separated and follows its own processing; it's dried and used as fuel for the mill. Ninety percent of the bagasse at Cora Texas is burned, Charlie told me: "we produce half of our electricity from bagasse." Much of the rest becomes the basis for a product made by another onsite company that creates small, shiny black pellets, an environmentally friendly substitute for coal. But some dried bagasse inevitably escapes as dust, coating every staircase and handrail in the factory.

The cane juice is clarified in six tall boilers, each the diameter of a backyard kiddie pool. Coagulant is added, and after a complicated process, the mud is separated from the juice and is returned to the fields. "We've got to recover everything," Adrian explained.

The juice is filtered further, then evaporated in twelve fat metal cylinders as tall as two-story buildings. The gauges and pipes plastered on their exterior surface reveal what is happening inside if you know how to read them. Adrian, of course, does, and removes a glass tube from a pipe, wipes the dark liquid onto a glass slide, and peers at it. I could see that small crystals had formed. Still 75 percent water, 25 percent syrup, he pronounced, not there yet, and invited me to dip my finger in. But, yes, it tasted good enough for pancakes.

The next suite of machines is comprised of the vacuum pans that heat the syrup and evaporate the rest of the liquid from the crystals. The sloshy matter, called massecuite, enters centrifuges that move at the dizzying speed of one hundred revolutions per minute, spinning the molasses away. In this way, Cora Texas produces nine million gallons of molasses annually, which is sold to a manufacturer of animal feed.

Minus the molasses, the centrifuge walls become caked with a thick, grainy coating the color of cornmeal—the raw sugar. It's scraped from the centrifuge walls onto conveyor belts and carried to the floor of a mammoth warehouse, then unceremoniously dumped onto a small, tawny-colored mountain already in place. The floor of the cavernous warehouse is carpeted with a layer of these sticky, one-millimeter grains of perfect, pale-gold, raw sugar crystals. As I pick my way across the floor to see the small mountain close up, I can hear the crunching of sugar crystals underfoot.

The raw sugar will be hauled to a refinery across the river to be made into table sugar. This happens all year, not just in grinding season, I was surprised to learn. "We ship sugar to the refinery every day, except holidays," Charlie informed me.

I left the mill, through the muddy lot, with sticky shoe soles and significant respect for the sweetener in my coffee.

When I happened to pass Cora Texas a few months later, no

ethereal pennants of steam rose above the stack; the letters on the tall column were perfectly legible. No gridlock of eighteen-wheelers crowded the lot around the mill; instead, a few men washed trucks, and the perimeter was ringed with empty basket trailers. I pulled into the lot and listened. The last sugar mill on the River Road was very, very quiet. Grinding season had ended. 'Til next year.

12

The Forgotten Fort

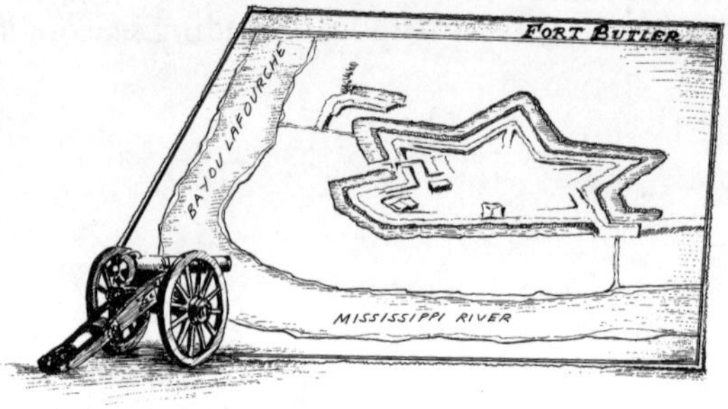

Civil War buffs wander with great dedication through historic battlefields and parks commemorating the War Between the States. But somehow, the site of Fort Butler, the only Civil War fort along the Mississippi River between New Orleans and Baton Rouge, is not usually part of their itinerary. Its location is, admittedly, a bit understated these days—an open, grassy field that folds onto the broad flank of the levee, with nothing visible to reveal what happened here save words on two granite monuments and a formidable black cannon on wheels.

A third, more prominent marker has nothing to do with the Civil War. It recognizes the importance of the Lemann Pumping Station, the top of which can be seen just over the levee. Its incised lettering informs visitors that the station was created in 1955 to restore a flow of fresh water from the Mississippi River to Bayou Lafourche. This was significant because the bayou had historically connected to the river, making this confluence valuable for commerce and trade and the reason why the town of Donaldsonville had been established just across the bayou.

It was also the reason why the Union army had decided to build their star-shaped earthen fort here.

The Civil War monuments and the cannon do commemorate, if offhandedly, the battle that took place in July of 1863. One stone pays tribute to the brave Confederate troops who attacked the Union fort; the other honors the African Americans who had been inside the fort, although the role of the latter remains a source of contention among historians. Did the African Americans serve as Union soldiers, or were they merely Union support staff inside the fort?

These are academic arguments, but they may have generated the most interest shown in Fort Butler and its battle in recent times. Somehow, the story of the Battle of Fort Butler seems to have been largely lost, among both aficionados of the Civil War and locals. Fort Butler barely merits a footnote in most writing about the war; even the comprehensive Civil War Sites Advisory Commission of the National Park Service lists Donaldsonville, not Fort Butler, among Louisiana's twenty-three Civil War sites. And when I write this, no historic marker celebrates the site.

I have learned that the Battle of Fort Butler was just a skirmish, certainly eclipsed by the larger, nearby confrontations at Baton Rouge and Port Hudson. Furthermore, the notable Battle of Gettysburg happened to conclude at the same time guns blazed at Fort Butler. Nevertheless, I became curious why this unique site along the River Road appears to have been so utterly discounted and seemingly overlooked.

In August 1862, Union admiral David Farragut sent a letter to the secretary of the navy complaining that the citizens of Donaldsonville "have pursued a uniform practice of firing upon our steamers." Farragut had warned residents to stop, he wrote his superior. Despite his threat to destroy the town, however, Confederate loyalists had persisted in firing cannons from town wharves as Union boats steamed up the river. Finally, after the citizens fired on the Union steamboat *Laurel Hill,* killing the pilot and wounding crew members, Farragut warned the good citizens of Donaldsonville to remove their women and children, for he was about to bombard them. The townspeople seemed skeptical that even their sworn enemy would fire on a town with a convent and orphanage sited so close to the river.

Donaldsonville was a town with an illustrious history, dating—in a way—back to a Chitimacha settlement noted by Iberville, and to eighteenth-century Acadian farmers who had colonized the area. In 1806, Englishman William Donaldson had formally developed the town referred to by the French as "La Ville de Donaldson."

Despite this pedigree, Federal gunboats blasted away at Donaldsonville for several hours, then sent a landing party to torch the town's remaining riverfront buildings "from the bayou to the church," according to their orders. Only seven buildings survived intact as the admiral wrote his senior officer, "I fulfilled my promise to a certain extent." The parish of Ascension agreed to stop shelling Federal ships, and Yankee regiments then moved into what was left of the little community. In a black-and-white photograph of the era, two Federal schooners are docked next to the rubble-strewn wharves of the town front.

Union forces had already captured both New Orleans and Baton Rouge, but Vicksburg and Port Hudson had not yet fallen. That made Donaldsonville strategic along the Mississippi, and its location on a bayou, usually navigable by steamboat, offered a back route to the Gulf of Mexico. The Union army confiscated private property on the upriver side of Bayou Lafourche and fronting the Mississippi in the even smaller town of Port Barrow. There they began construction of the fortification.

Fort Butler was named for Gen. Benjamin Butler, who was hated by the Confederate population, making the garrison even more of an insult. Construction was so nearly finished in January 1863 that the Federal officer in command reported he thought them ready to resist five thousand assailants, with backup from gunboats. Liberated plantation slaves had helped build the star-shaped fort, its solid walls fashioned from mud brick and possibly bricks salvaged from destroyed buildings in town. A substantial, brick-lined moat with sharpened sticks placed upright on its floor provided extra defense.

The star shape, a common configuration, allowed defending troops to observe and counter attacks from every direction. At Fort Butler, these might include assailants from both waterways, so the fort perimeter was also protected with stockade wings into both channels. Seven 24-pounder siege cannons and a 30-pounder cannon were positioned inside.

At the center of the enclosure, Union troops erected an 80-foot flagpole with a crow's nest halfway up to serve as a lookout. Local citizens were commanded to attend the fort's dedication on February 9, 1863, when Maj. Joseph Bullen ordered the Union flag run up the pole. After "The Star-Spangled Banner" was played and cannons fired a salute, the Confederates present were warned that anyone contemplating resistance, or even pulling down the flag, "will be shot on the spot."

A single known black-and-white photograph of Fort Butler shows a wide and dusty lot on which sits a small collection of simple wooden buildings and sheds. The famed flagpole is not in evidence, but several horse-drawn carts with seated passengers stand at the ready. A man on horseback approaches and two women, their backs to the camera, gaze at the activity around them as they stand atop a narrow wooden pontoon bridge laid across Bayou Lafourche. The solid construction of the Mississippi levee rises in the background, ending to reveal a visible arc of river. Behind the levee rise peaked roofs of perhaps a house and barn. When the photo is compared to an 1880 diagrammatic of Donaldsonville, Port Barrow, and Fort Butler produced by the Army Corps of Engineers, it appears that the iconic photograph may actually have been taken on fort property but not within the earthen walls.

In late June 1863, Confederate general Thomas Green of Texas was assigned to lead two brigades toward Fort Butler, part of planned attacks to prevent the Union from retaining their strongholds on the Mississippi, especially those with access to bayous. The Union forces within Fort Butler seem to have been apprised of Green's approach. Local lore tells of a heroic young Yankee soldier who volunteered to sneak off through darkness to the Confederates' camp and learn their plans. Somehow, he made it through the picket lines and returned with the intel.

The attack on Fort Butler came shortly thereafter, at 1:00 a.m. on June 28.

General Green had camped along Bayou Lafourche, well above the fort, and had constructed a bridge across the bayou so troops could approach down both banks. Others would advance from upriver along the Mississippi. Additional cavalry and rangers were to attack separately. The plan was to surround the fort, cross the moats, and shoot the cannoneers. Had the plan gone as proposed, Confederate soldiers might have overwhelmed the two hundred defenders inside the fort before Union gunboats could begin firing. They had counted on the gunboats not reacting if their compatriots were taken captive. But the gunboats were signaled as the enemy approached and began shelling.

Furthermore, the men in gray hadn't appreciated the complicated structure of the fort. Although they managed to breach some of the outer walls, they were ultimately stymied by the moats. Confederate and Union soldiers were reduced to hurling chunks of brick at each other. After three and a half hours of intense fighting, the support from four Federal gunboats moored in the river swayed the battle's outcome. The Federal forces in the fort were victorious; numerous Confederates fled in the dark. The remaining Rebel soldiers were forced to surrender.

Dawn revealed a grisly scene of dead and wounded soldiers strewn about the grounds of the fort and plots of earth scorched by cannon fire. Tents and wagons were smoldering. However, the numbers of dead and wounded at the Battle of Fort Butler differed according to who told the story. A contemporary article from the *New York Herald* called the battle a "murderous affair" in which the enemy (the Confederates) suffered a loss of over 100 men with 120 taken prisoner; the Union, it reported, had lost only 5 men with 14 wounded. But Confederate records reported 40 men dead, 114 wounded, and 107 missing (which probably included those who had fled). Union corpses were transported to the National Cemetery at Chalmette, south of New Orleans, for burial; dead Confederates were buried in unmarked graves on the grounds outside the fort.

Federal troops remained at Fort Butler through the Civil War and Reconstruction, then departed. The United States Army briefly returned to reactivate the fort in 1898 during the Spanish-American War, in case it should be needed. It was not.

Thereafter, Fort Butler was permanently abandoned. Its earthworks remained intact until 1903 when they were "recycled" as construction material for a permanent dam across Bayou Lafourche and as dirt to enlarge the levee.

The Battle of Fort Butler seemed of little import in Donaldsonville (perhaps because the Confederates lost?) until local Civil War buffs formed the nonprofit Fort Butler Foundation. They wanted to guarantee that the skirmish and the fort would have a place in local and state history. To this end, in 1996, the foundation sponsored an archaeological dig in cooperation with the Louisiana Division of Archaeology. This involved much negotiation with the Corps of Engineers because history was buried so close to the toe of the levee. Ultimately, the dig unearthed long-forgotten sections of Fort Butler's brick-lined moat, part of an arched brick entrance to the powder magazine, and several other brick foundations. Some buttons, minié balls, and a smattering of other relics of life at the fort were also uncovered, but archaeologists conjectured that most of the artifacts from the Civil War era had probably disappeared when the fort's bricks and earth walls were removed to dam the bayou.

Two years after the excavation, Andrew Capone and Glenn Falgoust, principals in the Fort Butler Foundation, set about to convince Louisiana leaders to make the hallowed ground of Fort

Butler a state historic site. A contingent of interested state legislators accepted their invitation to visit this place where "black Union soldiers rallied to defeat the Confederate assault." It represented, the legislators were told, one of the first major battles of the Civil War in which African American soldiers played a role—where black hands had not only constructed this citadel of freedom but also defended it.

And here was where disagreements arose as professional historians such as Craig Bauer questioned whether African American troops had actually been part of the fighting force at Fort Butler. Union military reports from the battle, he said, made no mention of African Americans; nor does the only eyewitness report from inside the fort. African Americans were definitely present in the fort, he knew, but they might have been convalescing from previous skirmishes or serving as orderlies, helping care for wounded soldiers. However, Bauer added, African Americans were certainly part of the crews of the Union gunboats that shelled the Confederate assault on the fort.

The state demurred and would not assume control of the Fort Butler site, which was nevertheless added to the National Register of Historic Places. To date, however, there is little to show for this designation. Save the two granite monuments and a cannon, the scene remains a greensward sloping up to the levee, although the several undefined hillocks disrupting otherwise smooth terrain probably mark the remnants of disturbed earth from the archaeological excavation. The most prominent feature of the site is the steep white-shell drive that climbs the levee slope to the pumping station that hums loudly as it pushes water from the Mississippi River through underground pipes to Bayou Lafourche, a mile to the west.

I've seen an aerial view of the area with the star-shaped outline of the fort superimposed on the contemporary landscape. The long back wall of the fort traces the line of the Mississippi River levee; the points of the star cover an area where buildings and roads now exist in Port Barrow, considered a suburb of Donaldsonville. This diagram enabled me to envision everything I'd read about, prompting me to wonder why at least this visual of Fort Butler could not be engraved on a granite monument and placed next to the existing three. Then Civil War buffs, and curious people like me, could remember and understand the story of what happened here.

13

The Mysterious Mound by the Side of the Road

About four miles upriver from the tiny community of Darrow on the east bank of the River Road is a straight section of highway. This is unusual along this narrow, curving roadway, so it is easy to speed by and fail to notice a rusty chain-link fence. Interlaced with untamed trees and shrubs, the fence traces the river side of the road for about a quarter of a mile and turns inward on the upriver end, to run parallel to the base of the levee. An aerial view of the plot shows this tract to have the shape of a trapezium.

Inside the fence is an earthen plateau that stands about as high as my shoulder. It is quite visible from the road if you stop to look—a mysterious formation, too low and oddly shaped for an Indian mound, too contrived to be a natural outcropping in this low, flat landscape.

At one time, a small white sign with black lettering pronounced the identity of the place: OLD INGER OIL SITE. Since the sign is no longer there, however, passersby might presume that this tangle of vegetation and unidentified dirt is abandoned, just another derelict area along a roadway that has too many of them. Or one might assume it is some kind of natural preserve, where dainty, bicolored wild violets smile up from the dirt among a carpet of dandelions and blackberry thickets and where, if you stop, unseen birds are heard chirping and the chipping of frogs and crickets is loud. One day I watched a hawk swirl overhead.

The bold, red-lettered admonishment wired to a locked gate at the downriver end immediately refutes this possibility, however. Only authorized personnel may enter, it reads, and only under the auspices of the Louisiana Department of Environmental Quality. This is clearly no garden spot. It is, although the sign doesn't say so, a former Superfund site, once one of the most toxic and contaminated places in the country. Now it is remediated, neutralized as much as science can achieve, and holds no danger but must forever be fenced off and made inaccessible to visitors.

And yet, I'd argue, Old Inger deserves identification, even some explication about what it is, for in its way, this industrial relic is as much a part of the history and culture along the River Road as the loveliest of antebellum mansions.

The story of the mystery mound began in 1967 when the Darrow Oil Company established a small factory here to process used oil. They would buy waste oils from refineries and businesses that performed automobile oil changes, haul it to the River Road facility on trucks or by barge, and store the fluids in holding tanks until processing. After Darrow Oil's specialized machinery removed impurities from the oil, it was to be stored onsite until purchased. Unbeknownst to Darrow Oil, however, some of the waste oils the company purchased contained hazardous materials that couldn't be separated from the base oil, making this product unmarketable. Their solution was to dig holding ponds enclosed with earthen dams (known in the business as "lagoons") in which to store the contaminated oil until a solution could be found for its disposal. When no long-term plan for this problem materialized, the lagoons occasionally were pumped so full that Darrow Oil was forced to siphon excess liquid sludge into an adjacent swamp.

In 1978, a large spill occurred when nine storage tanks of unprocessed oil overflowed into the lagoons and the swamp, despoiling the land on which Darrow Oil Refinery sat. The company then sold the site to the Old Inger Oil Refinery.

Old Inger intended to clean up the toxic land and restart the refinery. They were not, however, model operators, according to Wilma Subra. Wilma is an award-winning and no-nonsense environmental consultant and activist. She remembered Old Inger as "badly operated . . . sloppy with emissions and flares, very smelly." Soon enough, Old Inger's refinery structures and tanks were coated in oily material from overflows. Toxic seepage contaminated local groundwater, and the air smelled of rotten eggs. Approximately two hundred residents living within a mile radius of the site complained of breathing problems. "When the wind blew," Wilma recalled, "the smell wafted for a couple of miles around . . . through the neighborhood, and even across the river."

The new owners realized that cleaning up the site would prove much more expensive than they had reckoned, so, in 1981, they simply abandoned their investment. They walked away from fourteen acres covered with almost two million gallons of toxic waste fluids that could easily seep beyond the boundaries of their property.

I never saw Old Inger then, but photographs from that time are chilling. The worst one shows a sludgy, oily lagoon, its surface black and dotted with metal barrels slimy with oil. The lagoon is surrounded by skeletons of dead trees and shrubs. The site had "open pits, drains, waste oil slops and a marsh area—the lagoons—filled with oil waste percolating," Dr. Ralph Portier affirmed. He remembered no living trees or other vegetation, "just lots of black, gunky, oily fluid and it smelled like fresh asphalt." Two hundred nefarious-sounding substances were identified, with names like diphenylhydrazine, nitrosodiphenylamine, naphthalene, dichlorophenol, and nitrophenol benzidine. Nevertheless, cows grazed nearby and locals crawfished in the ditches by the road; this easy accessibility to people, animals and vehicles presented an additional danger.

Ralph Portier is a portly and enthusiastic microbiologist and toxicologist at Louisiana State University in whose lab was invented the heroic stew of microbes that counteracted the toxic compounds identified at Old Inger. His team might be called the heroes of the mystery mound since the acreage within the rusty chain-link fence gained national significance as the first Superfund site to use bioremediation for cleanup.

"Superfund" is a designation established in 1980 to indicate a site of extreme and hazardous toxicity. The Superfund program was created through a federal act referred to as CERCLA (the Comprehensive Environmental Response, Compensation, and Liability Act) and overseen by the Environmental Protection Agency (EPA). It was innovative at the time, identifying sites that had reached a significantly dangerous level of contamination and offered substantial threat to human health, the environment, or both. The Superfund legislation also broke new legal ground by acknowledging the public's right to know about the existence of such places. This aspect of the law came in response to the egregious case of Love Canal in New York State, where a school and housing development had been constructed on part of an unidentified hazardous waste site, resulting in extensive and extraordinary health problems for children and adults. The Superfund act also allocated funding to be used by the government to clean up a site when the responsible parties could not be found. These cases tallied a bit more than 30 percent of their roster; Old Inger was among them.

This was in the day, Wilma Subra reminded me, when "there were fewer rules and regulations about hazardous materials and much less concern about environmental conditions" than today. The cleanup of Old Inger occurred early in the history of the Superfund program. It was a new environmental effort, and "Edwin Edwards [Louisiana governor at the time] didn't want the stigma of a Superfund site" here, Wilma remembered.

Nevertheless, in 1983, the Louisiana Environmental Control Commission (predecessor to the Louisiana Department of Environmental Quality) formally declared Old Inger abandoned. This entitled the site to placement on the National Priorities List, defining the most hazardous and contaminated places known in the country, which was used to guide the EPA in determining where and whether to take action.

The EPA awarded Louisiana funding to investigate the type and extent of contamination and to conduct a feasibility study to identify options for remedial action. The usual way to detoxify such places was either to excavate the hazardous materials and poisoned soil and truck them to a landfill, or bury them in a large, concrete-lined tomb. Neither option was viable at the Old Inger site, however, because it was too close to the levee. Both the Corps of Engineers and the supervisory Pontchartrain Levee District feared that either action could undermine the levee. And, with the water table in south Louisiana so close to the surface, digging a secure burial vault was additionally problematic.

As it happened, Ralph Portier was engaged with a federal grant to investigate the new technology of bioremediation, in its infancy in the 1980s. "We were one of only two or three groups in the country doing this," he told me. His research focused on how microorganisms could be used to degrade a variety of hazardous wastes. Microbes exist naturally in soil, water, and air, too small to be detected without a microscope. Some had been found to be "metabolically talented"—able to break down metals, acids, salt, methane, even radioactive wastes. In layperson's terms, the technology of bioremediation involved analyzing the contaminants of the hazardous waste, classifying its variety of chemicals, then concocting a mix of microorganisms known to have the capability to target and degrade them. "I had to prove the concept, to prove it could be done, and then provide the recipe to do it," he explained. "It took a lot of convincing." Only then would the EPA allow the use of bioremediation at Old Inger.

Compounds from all the affected areas—aboveground holding tanks, waste burials, manmade lagoons, the swamp—were brought to Dr. Portier's lab for analysis. The first step was to determine the ingredients in the various toxic stews and then test to see which microbes could neutralize them. He also had to estimate how long the process would take. It could be a bit like composting in a garden, he said with a cheerful smile. The introduced microbes would stay at the site, continually working, until there was no more (toxic) waste for them to eat.

At his LSU lab, Dr. Portier banked his microbes in a large archival library. The microbes were all living, kept as discrete samples in separate ampules, permanently frozen at 185 degrees Centigrade but able to be revived.

Ultimately, the solution for remediating Old Inger involved constructing a large liner like a giant swimming pool, with barrier walls made of packed virgin clay three or four feet thick. The clay, hauled in from another location, was selected for being impervious to seepage and able to trap and block heavy metals so they could not escape. Within the aboveground "swimming pool" (the mystery mound formation), Dr. Portier's lab created a land farm, with layers of waste, then layers of microbes, spread within the impermeable walls. "You put down a treatment layer, add fresh soil, till, fertilize, and treat." One layer was allowed to degrade before another layer was added.

The microbes reduced the organic waste and allowed the metals in the stew to be immobilized and concentrated. Microbes don't specifically interact with metals, Dr. Portier explained, but do change their solubility. The clay used for the "swimming pool" at Old Inger bound the metals, effectively rendering them immobile. This process became a common way to treat such metals at many subsequent Superfund sites.

The bonus to Dr. Portier's bioremediation done onsite was that it proved considerably less expensive than alternatives. And he felt very rewarded by the project: "It was important to me both scientifically and personally [to make sure] that nothing would be endangered in the future" by Old Inger. "I did not want to create another Love Canal."

The bioremediation was considered successful enough, within the margins of safety, that in 2006 the name of the Old Inger Oil Refinery was removed from the National Register of Extraordinarily Toxic Tracts—as I've nicknamed the official Superfund roster. Now, Old Inger must be monitored and regularly inspected every five years, forever, to assure the state, and nearby River Road residents, that the clay container is secure. One problem to watch for is trees growing on the top of the mound; their roots could undermine the integrity of the clay cap.

Old Inger is still located right next to the River Road; anyone can stop, approach its perimeter, and peer through the fence. If you do, you will see only an elevated dirt form, much higher than the land on the other side of the road. You will see a flat expanse on which native shrubs, weeds, and wildflowers have taken root. Perhaps a hawk will fly overhead and you can hear the chipping of frogs. And you will know to be very grateful.

14
Shall We Thank Mr. Rosenwald?

Kathe Hambrick believes there is a definite link between the early-twentieth-century CEO of Sears Roebuck, Julius Rosenwald, and the small frame building that now sits on a quiet corner in a run-down but historic area of Donaldsonville. Not that the Chicago multimillionaire had ever visited the building—a school—but because it might have been part of a unique program Rosenwald started, a program critical to the education of thousands of rural African American children.

Her challenge was to make the link real because, if she could, that would make the little building even more historic than she knew it was.

The clean-lined little structure, fondly remembered as the old Central Elementary School, was originally located in the tiny community of Central in east-bank St. James Parish. Black children in grades one through eight attended the school from 1931 until the 1960s. Kathe, founder and longtime director of the River Road African American Museum, had a mission to tell the history and contributions of African Americans along the River Road. Central Elementary was an important piece of that community's experience and cultural legacy. So it seemed logical to save the derelict building when it was destined for demolition.

She believed it warranted saving for another reason, too. The Central Elementary building looked suspiciously like one of the famous Rosenwald Schools. And, if it actually was a Rosenwald, it would be one of only three such schools remaining in Louisiana. At one time, there had been four hundred in the state, educating one quarter of all black elementary students. After integration in the 1960s, however, many Rosenwald buildings were abandoned, became ravaged by time, and were eventually torn down. Others were sold and altered beyond recognition. In fact, Rosenwald Schools were so threatened nationally that, in 2002, the National Trust for Historic Preservation listed them among that year's roster of most-endangered historic places.

So Central Elementary deserved to be saved for one good reason, and possibly two.

The Rosenwald School program was created as the result of an unusual partnership between businessman Julius Rosenwald and African American leader Booker T. Washington. Rosenwald, the son of a German immigrant and a self-made man, harbored deep instincts for social justice. He had already read Booker T. Washington's autobiography, *Up from Slavery,* when the black author and educator arrived in Chicago in 1910 to give a public talk. Washington was then president of the all-black Tuskegee Institute, an Alabama institution begun in 1881 as a teacher-training program. When Tuskegee first opened, Washington told his audiences, class was conducted in a shanty and the school's assembly space was provided by a nearby church. If it rained while he was teaching, a student held an umbrella over his head. But Washington's energy and leadership had transformed Tuskegee into a vibrant college with excellent facilities and a curriculum expanded far beyond teaching teachers. Among the strong faculty he attracted was the first black architect to graduate from the Massachusetts Institute of Technology's prestigious architecture program.

Booker T. Washington and Julius Rosenwald became fast friends, and the college president invited the philanthropist to join Tuskegee's board of directors. According to legend, Rosenwald asked Washington what was needed for black students and Washington quickly responded, "We need education for blacks in the rural South." And this became the catalyst for the formation of one of the most progressive educational initiatives in the country.

The Rosenwald Schools began in 1912 with a pilot program of six elementary schools built near Tuskegee. When they proved successful, the two founders began to scale up, relying on an unusual funding formula they devised that would today be called matching grants. Julius Rosenwald agreed to donate one-third of the money needed to build a good schoolhouse, the district school board was required to contribute one-third, and the black community whose students would enroll at the school was responsible for the final third. Tuskegee would furnish blueprints.

The communities in which the schools would be built were poor, and they scrabbled together funds from church collections and fraternal lodges, by staging rallies, hosting picnics, and sponsoring entertainments. Their contribution could be cash and/or in-kind, so locals often contributed sweat equity—cutting lumber for construction and actually building the schoolhouse themselves.

The plans for the schools were created by Tuskegee's architectural students and faculty. In 1915, Tuskegee published a handbook called *The Negro Rural School* that defined the architectural principles required in a Rosenwald School, to create an environment conducive to student learning. Templates evolved.

The conventional Rosenwald School design presented a single-story building fabricated of wood and raised on piers to enhance ventilation. The plain gable roof had small windows on the gable ends to aid circulation; a north-south orientation of the building avoided direct sunlight into the classrooms. But the interior was well lit by batteries of double-hung windows that also provided fresh air. Transoms were installed above interior doorways, and ceilings were constructed twelve or fourteen feet high to enhance air circulation. Sliding doors between rooms created flexible spaces; movable blackboards allowed teachers to reconfigure their classrooms so that each school felt airy and welcoming.

Today, in this era of increased environmental awareness, the Rosenwald Schools have merited accolades from the Louisiana Green Building Council. The nonprofit that promotes sustainable building recognized the designs of Rosenwald Schools—some built nearly a century ago—as remarkably "green." Through their placement of windows, doors, and transoms and their use of natural light, the architects at Tuskegee had thoughtfully addressed the climate of the rural South and the needs of the children and teachers who would occupy the buildings.

The schoolhouses were painted both inside and out according to a defined palette. Facades might be brown with white trim, white with gray trim, or light gray with white trim; interior rooms could have walnut- or oak-stained wainscoting, walls of gray or buff, ceilings painted light cream or ivory. (Some of the paint came directly from Sears stores' paint departments—either purchased or donated.) With their pleasing appearance and vital function of educating young African Americans, the Rosenwald Schools became a source of pride in local communities. When a school burned—sometimes quite mysteriously—area residents usually rebuilt it.

Rosenwald Schools were categorized according to the number of teachers they employed rather than by their square footage. The smallest school was a one-teacher unit; the largest was a four-teacher school. Central Elementary was one of the latter, recalled Varie Stewart, who attended Central in the early 1950s. The school's four teachers taught in separate classrooms, each room serving two grades: first and second grades together; third with fourth; fifth with sixth; and seventh with eighth.

After Booker T. Washington's death in 1915, Julius Rosenwald realized the need for closer oversight and better organization of the program. He moved it under the wing of his Julius Rosenwald Fund, a private nonprofit he had founded to aid his philanthropic work, and also opened a southern office dedicated to rural southern schools.

The Sears magnate died in 1932, never truly knowing the enduring success of Rosenwald Schools that continued until school integration. Between 1912 and 1932, almost five thousand schools were built in fifteen southern states; more than six hundred thousand black children passed through their doors. The Rosenwald program had also constructed ancillary buildings near their schools, including teachers' homes and workshops.

In Louisiana, one-quarter of black schools were Rosenwald affiliates. A handful were located along the River Road—at Armant, Edgard, Killona, Modeste, Plaquemine, Port Allen, and Reserve. Although none of these survive, they are listed in the definitive Fisk University database that annotates recognized Rosenwald Schools. Central Elementary is not included.

But this may not mean anything, Jeanne Cyriaque argued. Jeanne is a consultant about Rosenwald Schools and the former African American program coordinator at the Division of Historic Preservation in Georgia. She knew of other schools—definitely Rosenwalds—that had somehow been excluded from the database. And after she saw Central Elementary, she had few doubts.

"It's definitely a four-teacher Rosenwald plan," she affirmed, with all the bones of an authentic Rosenwald, and with a typical design and architectural elements. She noted Central's one-story frame construction raised on short brick piers, with a simple gable roof. The interior, though now well-worn, is light and airy with high ceilings and large, double-hung windows across the front and rear facades. Every door is crowned with an ample transom and, when I prowled the building on a warm day with Kathe Hambrick, I noticed that the building was comfortable enough. The rooms were not the least bit stuffy after she had opened only the doors, and it had no air conditioning.

Old Central Elementary's interior is decorated with plain wainscoting and chair rails with batten walls to the ceiling. It appeared to be divided into three rooms—two smaller ones on each side of the small front foyer and a long, open space at the rear. But Kathe showed me the sleeves of pocket doors remaining which, when closed, would have created two classrooms and, when opened, created a larger space that Varie Stewart remembered well. Sometimes a stage had been set up at one end for special programs, graduations, and community gatherings, and "it's where we wrapped a beautiful Maypole every year," she reminisced.

Varie also recalled sitting at long desks "with two on seat," which helps account for how two grade levels could share a classroom. The students ate lunch at their desks, cooked in a small kitchen separated from the room by a curtain. She remembered a wood-burning stove at each end of the long room to furnish heat; the holes for their exhaust remain today.

Central Elementary, it appears, was constructed exactly as the plans for a typical Rosenwald School would have dictated.

Clues to what may have happened regarding the school are revealed in several letters from 1931 exchanged between the Rosenwald Fund and education leaders in Louisiana. The Rosenwald Fund wrote the St. James Parish School Board to request the return of an appropriation. The letter did not specify whether misallocation had taken place or the money was simply never distributed. In a separate letter, the Rosenwald Fund wrote that it had accepted the return of the money "on four buildings never completed which will be expunged from our record, including the one in St. James Parish."

"So many cases like Central Elementary [occurred] where the governing authority reallocated the money," Jeanne Cyriaque suggested. What seems most probable in this case is that the black community kept the blueprints, or had committed them to memory, and built the school independently of both the formal Rosenwald program and the St. James Parish School Board. Central Elementary was a four-teacher Rosenwald plan, but not officially a Rosenwald School.

After integration, the building was repurposed as Romeville High School for Boys, where black and white young men attended together; girls were educated in a separate facility. After a large, new area high school was built, the old Central schoolhouse then became home to a Head Start program. By the mid-1990s, Head Start had decamped, leaving the building vacant.

When the school board made plans to demolish the derelict structure, Kathe asked them to donate it to her museum. They agreed to do so in 1997, but it took a long four years before she and her museum board could raise sufficient funding to move the building across the river to museum property. Then, before renovation could begin, transforming the historic schoolhouse into exhibit space and a place for community gatherings, several unexpected expenses arose. The blueprints had to be adjusted to suit new, post–Hurricane Katrina building codes; asbestos abatement had to be addressed.

The renovation began in earnest in 2013. Funds remaining after the surprise expenses were only sufficient to refurbish and repaint the exterior, refit original windows with new panes and muntin bars, and add a new tin roof. Shell Chemical donated new electrical wiring, and workers began to scrape the interior surfaces, seeking to determine what the historic paint colors might have been before the added layers from Head Start and Romeville High School for Boys.

And then, the money dried up. The schoolhouse interior had not yet been renovated or temperature controls installed. It was unusable for community gatherings, and no exhibits had been organized.

"I probably should never have moved the building," Kathe

lamented as she surveyed the half-completed project. The community who valued the old school had been in St. James Parish. "People [there] in their eighties protested about our moving the building," she opined. "They had pride in the school, even though they didn't know anything about the Rosenwald program." Few people in Donaldsonville or elsewhere seemed interested.

Conversely, however, if she hadn't moved the schoolhouse, it would certainly have been torn down, lost forever, since no other group had attempted to protect it. And that had added another challenge to attracting funding: by physically moving the schoolhouse, she had disqualified it from listing on the National Register of Historic Places. Although this designation has no legal standing, it often adds preservation cachet.

Cachet or not, after visiting the old building several times as well as looking at photographs of Rosenwald Schools in other parts of the South and reading about the program, I, like Kathe, am convinced of the link between Julius Rosenwald and old Central Elementary. All that seems to be missing today as I write this is the return of the same spirit and pride that built the schoolhouse in the 1930s.

I hope the renovation will be completed and that the programming envisioned for the old building will once again fill it with the same energy that Varie Stewart remembered. Then the entire River Road community can thank Mr. Rosenwald, at least for the inspiration . . .

ACKNOWLEDGMENTS

When I approached LSU Press with the idea of writing a second collection of River Road stories, I was pleased to be encouraged to do so. But I soon discovered that this undertaking, like the first *River Road Rambler,* was challenging. Because I wanted these stories to include information derived not only from archival research but also from interviews with knowledgeable people, I had to identify and track them down, which was no easy task. I am delighted to report, however, that, when I did, they were unfailingly helpful.

I am grateful to the following people who either served as resources or helped me learn about their subject matter. Without them, this would have been a different and, I think, less interesting book.

Thank you indeed to: Dennis Jones, David Floyd, and Kim Ginn; Kathe Hambrick, Jeanne Cyriaque, Varie Stewart, and Sullan Cloudet; Kevin Hardy and Bobby Otterstetter; John Ruskey, Charlie and Shirley Poche, and Jordan Hanssen; Stan Richardson and Richard Trepagnier; Michael Saucier; Norman and Sand Marmillion; Charlie Schudmak and Adrian Monge; Andrew Capone, Glenn Falgoust, and Craig Bauer; Wilma Subra, Ralph Portier, and Margaret Reams; Tim Murphy, Camilla Pugh, and Susan Illis; Robert Munson, Stephanie Smith, Jeff Kindl, and Scott Richardson; Ashley Rodgers, John Cummings, Woodrow Nash, and Rev. Ferdinand Gaines; and Brendan Rush.

Thanks also to Renee Pierce and Ron Boudreaux, who were happy to go adventuring.

I am also most grateful to the helpful librarians at the Louisiana State Library, the Iberville Parish and St. John Parish libraries, and the LSU Libraries. The latter provided not only primary and secondary source material from shelves and archives but also access to digital resources, allowing me to often research from the comfort of my home. It is truly remarkable to be able to read journal articles in JSTOR and old newspaper stories from *Chronicling America* while in my bathrobe.

I am indebted to LSU Press, whose professional staff produces consistently high-quality books, and especially to MaryKatherine Callaway, who allowed me to exceed my original deadline more than once, and to Catherine Kadair, my thoughtful editor.

And, as always, I am grateful to my family for inquiring about how my project was going and for cheering me on as I sometimes slogged, rather than skated, toward the goal of finishing this book. Thanks to family and friends for inspiration, constant support, and—I hope—your own pride in *River Road Rambler Returns.*